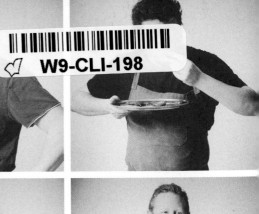

Individuels

Éclair	5²⁵
Chou à la crème	5⁵⁰
Chocolat, café St-Henri	6⁰⁰
Tartelette agrumes	6⁰⁰
Mousse fromage, pommes	6⁰⁰

Petits pots

Yogourt, ananas, muesli 5⁵⁰

Nos classiqu

Vert
Pot de c
Dessert

Rec

Chocolat

Chai L

Extra r

Montreal Cooks

Patrice
Patrice
Patrice
Patrice
Patrice
Patrice
Patrice
Patrice

A
Tasting Menu
FROM
THE CITY'S
LEADING
CHEFS

Montreal
Cooks

JONATHAN CHEUNG + TAYS SPENCER

foreword by Gail Simmons

Figure.1
Vancouver / Berkeley

Cataloguing data available from Library and Archives Canada
ISBN 978-1-927958-37-7 (hbk.)

Editing by Lucy Kenward
Copy editing by Grace Yaginuma
Index by Iva Cheung

Design by Jessica Sullivan
Photography by Fabrice Gaëtan, www.fabricegaetan.com

Printed and bound in China by C&C Offset Printing Co., Ltd.
Distributed in the U.S. by Publishers Group West

Figure 1 Publishing Inc.
Vancouver BC Canada
www.figure1pub.com

This book is dedicated to all the unsung
heroes in the restaurant industry who
help feed this amazing city of Montreal

⚜ Contents

Foreword

Full disclosure: I was born in Toronto.

There. I said it.

Still, my love affair with Montreal runs deep and dates back almost four decades. Actually, long before then. My grandfather Charlie arrived on the shores of the Saint Lawrence River from Poland in 1919 at the age of fourteen, and my grandmother Natasha emigrated from Russia in 1917. By the age of twenty-four, Charlie was a self-made man, running a garment company that sold affordable women's clothing during the Depression. They settled on avenue Pagnuelo and later moved to Westmount. My mother attended Roslyn School, Westmount High and then McGill, as did both of her older brothers. She grew up eating borscht and brisket at home, visited The Main for smoked meat and karnatzel, and learned to make bok choy and stir-fried noodles from a Chinese chef. Although she moved to Toronto in 1961, I've always believed she left her heart on Mount Royal, somewhere between Beaver Lake and Mile End.

Trips to visit my relatives in Montreal are among my very first memories. Those long drives in the back of our station wagon were bearable only with the knowledge that my uncle would be waiting to share with me a piece of local Quebec cheese he had bought that day at the Atwater Market, followed by a tarte Tatin from a little pastry shop on rue Sherbrooke I adored so much. As I got older, our meals in Montreal grew more anticipated. There was always an air of mystery and romance to the bistros we would visit, so different from the restaurants back home in Toronto, and where I could slurp up a piping hot bowl of onion soup gratinée or devour a plate of foie gras torchon accompanied by a perfectly crispy baguette. And for dessert, *pouding chômeur* of course. It was always the food that set the city apart for me;

put it on a pedestal; made me smile, as if it were winking.

It came as no surprise when I decided to attend McGill for university myself. Montreal held the most promise for fun, for excitement, for food. By my final year there, I realized it was eating that captured my interest more than any subject I was studying. I spent way more time cooking in my tiny apartment kitchen or visiting one of the countless ethnic restaurants downtown than I did at the library. It was at this time that I began writing about my restaurant experiences for the student paper, the *McGill Tribune*, never imagining those little articles about student-friendly (read: cheap) fondue joints on rue Prince Arthur or tiny cafés in the Plateau would lay the foundation for a lifetime of work in food media.

It was also no surprise when I moved to New York a few years later to pursue my culinary career and fell in love, not with a New York restaurateur or celebrity chef, but with a Montrealer. Of course he was wonderful in every way, although I had to admit that marrying him conveniently gave me the excuse I needed to return to the city on a regular basis. And so I have had the great pleasure of being able to come back several times a year, to see friends and family, but most of all to eat.

In the many years since I've lived and worked in New York, the restaurant scene in Montreal has evolved and blossomed enormously. It has produced, and fiercely protects, what I think is Canada's most distinct and creative cuisine—simple and rustic, layered and robust, intoxicating and playful—calling on the myriad cultures and ethnicities that make up its diverse population and mixing them with its French-Canadian roots. Of course the quality of produce, meat and dairy in Quebec certainly helps make the food so outstanding. But it's the chefs, who cook every day ignoring stereotypes and convention, taking risks while putting their heritage centre stage, making delicious, lustful food the only way they know how. Like Montrealers.

It's about time we had a cookbook that celebrated all of this, created with care, at just the right time: when Montreal chefs and restaurants are finally getting the recognition they deserve, for cooking some of the most outrageous, exciting, thought-provoking and fabulous food in the world. With *Montreal Cooks*, I will now have not only a definitive list of dishes to try on my next visit but the ability to bring these meals back to my own kitchen, to enjoy whenever my heart starts to ache for the flavours of home.

Je me souviens.

GAIL SIMMONS

Introduction

I grew up in the restaurant business. In fact, that's all I really know. When I was ten years old, running into the kitchen of my family's restaurant in Vancouver was probably the most exciting thing I could think of. Watching flames bursting out from underneath the woks, fish frying in vats of bubbling oil and huge pots of chowder simmering on the stove was my version of heaven.

I was lucky. From a very young age, I already knew that I wanted to be a cook. The kitchen was where the action was. It was where I saw chefs grinding away, night after night, creating deliciously beautiful dishes out of fresh raw ingredients. And where I first saw people eating and grinning with satisfaction after taking their first bite of a meal. It was that feeling that fuelled my passion: I don't cook to eat. I cook to feed. Watching people enjoy my food gives me much more joy than savouring exquisitely prepared meals myself.

Although my roots are in restaurants, I didn't truly discover my passion for all things food until I moved from Vancouver, via Hong Kong, to Montreal in 2004. This city is a special place. Almost like the perfect storm, it combines small, intimate spaces; access to some of the greatest food markets in North America; and creative chefs deeply rooted in their own culinary heritage. And the result is one of the most exciting and diverse restaurant scenes in the world. It's no wonder that so many chefs converge on Montreal for inspiration.

The food in this city can excite even the tamest of palates. The terroir of Quebec runs deep and provides some of the most unique ingredients around. Maple syrup, artisan cheeses, fresh duck and foie gras are just the tip of the iceberg. Venison from the Outaouais, seafood from the Gaspé and lamb from the Charlevoix are all regular standouts on the menus of Montreal's finest restaurants. Accompanying them are local seasonal products like fiddleheads and garlic scapes from some of the forty-five thousand independent farmers in the region, the vegetables treated with equal respect to the proteins on the plate.

But eating out in Montreal is not just about the food. It's the whole orchestra. On any given night at any given restaurant, Tays, my wife, and I are likely to run into friends or clients, chat with the chef about a new favourite cookbook and sip some of the finest wines the sommelier is excited about that day. But whether you live here or not, Montreal is one of the most electrifying places in the world to eat. Travelling to this city purely for food is surprisingly common. Tourists make a point of experiencing what they read about and see in the media. It's this joie de vivre, this convivial atmosphere, that makes Montreal and its restaurants such a wonderful place to eat.

Although I don't currently work in a traditional restaurant, having a shop like Appetite for Books has allowed me to meet many great cooks in this city. People in every aspect of the industry, from chefs de cuisine to dishwashers, have perused the shelves of the bookstore trying to find the right book or recipe. And after chatting with all these people about our shared passion for food, the experience of eating in their restaurants is even more special. So when you read through *Montreal Cooks* and meet the chefs behind some of my and

Tays's favourite restaurants, you can now get your own taste of Montreal—whether the food is prepared in their kitchen or your own.

Putting together this book has allowed Tays and me to relive our restaurant experiences and get the details about who is behind the meals we've shared in our nearly ten years of eating out together. It's also inspired us to be better cooks. The chefs featured here push boundaries with their ingredients, their flavour pairings and the techniques they use to prepare their dishes. Among their recipes, you'll encounter wintry meals and light summery ones, dishes that are quick to whip up and some that may challenge you. But we guarantee that anything you sample from this book will transport you to Montreal— in spirit, if not in person.

This city has a very long history as a culinary destination for food lovers not only within Canada but from around the world. The ritual of eating good food and enjoying life is second nature to Montrealers. Trends may change, tastes may evolve, but our culinary scene will forever be incomparable.

Tays and I always say that a good meal creates a great memory. So go make some great memories in your kitchen—and then come visit all of us in Montreal!

JONATHAN CHEUNG

The Recipes

Appetizers and Little Meals

Salads and Soups

Mains

Desserts and Sweets

Brunch

Preserves

Balsam Inn

— chef —

ERIC DUPUIS AND
DAVID CHAMPAGNE-LECLERC

Eric Dupuis is the original chef and co-owner of Dominion Square Tavern (page 43) in the Golden Square Mile at the base of Mount Royal in downtown Montreal. The success of that restaurant brought about the Balsam Inn, which opened in October 2014 just next door, in the former kitchen of the Dominion Square Hotel. Inspired by 1940s-era brasseries, the Balsam Inn features lots of wood, brass and a splendid fireplace used to prepare its signature flatbread. And the dining room, the impressively long bar and the restrooms are all exquisitely designed with details that transport us back to that era.

From the dining room, we like to peek through the industrial windows into the kitchen, where Eric and his chef de cuisine, David Champagne-Leclerc, create modest, mostly Mediterranean-inspired dishes. Their Pig's Trotter Savoury Cake is an ode to English tradition and a nod to the popularity of nose-to-tail dishes, while the orecchiette with clams showcases the kitchen's deft hand with pasta, confit tomatoes and fresh East Coast shellfish—all bright points on a cold Montreal winter's night.

facing PIG'S TROTTER SAVOURY CAKE

Tomato jam

1 lb fresh heirloom tomatoes
  (about 2 large)
½ lb (1 heaping cup) white sugar

Braised pig's trotters

4 pig's trotters
1 small onion, peeled
1 celery stalk
1 carrot
2 garlic cloves, unpeeled
2 bay leaves
4 sprigs fresh thyme

Pig's Trotter Savoury Cake

This cake is delicious at any time but is best served sliced, pan-seared and topped with a poached egg as a hangover brunch dish. Look for the smoked Caciocavallo cheese in good grocery stores, or substitute smoked mozzarella or smoked Gruyère instead. Start the tomato jam the day before you plan to serve this dish.

Tomato jam Cut the tomatoes into 1-inch pieces and place them in a large bowl. Add the sugar and stir gently until well mixed. Cover and refrigerate for 12 hours.

Have ready one 1-pint (2-cup) canning jar with a sealable lid. Bring a pot of water to a boil over high heat. Using tongs, place the jar, lid and sealing band into the boiling water and allow to simmer for at least 10 minutes. Transfer the sterilized jar and lid pieces to a dish rack to drain.

Pour the chilled tomato mixture into a large pot and bring to a boil over medium-high heat, stirring often so it doesn't burn. Reduce the heat to low and simmer for 10 to 15 minutes. Drop a spoonful onto a clean, room temperature plate. If the mixture has the consistency of thick, runny jam, it is ready. If it is still a bit liquid, allow it to simmer for another 5 minutes. Remove from the heat, allow to cool to room temperature and pour into the jar. Will keep refrigerated for up to 1 week.

Braised pig's trotters Place all the ingredients in a large pot, cover with cold water and bring to a boil over high heat. Reduce the heat to low, cover and simmer for 2 hours. Using tongs, transfer the trotters to a plate to cool for 15 minutes and

Savoury cake

3 large eggs

½ cup extra-virgin olive oil

½ cup milk

2 Tbsp Dijon mustard

1½ cups all-purpose flour

1 tsp baking powder

reserved pig's trotters (about
   1½ lbs meat)

1½ lbs smoked Caciocavallo
   cheese, grated

3 Tbsp chopped fresh parsley
   + sprigs for garnish

salt and pepper

1 Tbsp grapeseed oil (optional)

1 Tbsp melted butter (optional)

discard the cooking water. When the meat is cool enough to handle, pull the cooked flesh and cartilage off the bones with your hands. Set the meat aside in a bowl and discard the bones and cartilage.

Savoury cake Preheat the oven at 375°F. Lightly grease a 5 × 9-inch loaf pan.

In a bowl, mix together the eggs, olive oil, milk and mustard. In a separate bowl, sift together the flour and baking powder. Gradually stir the flour mixture into the egg mixture, mixing well with a wooden spoon. Add the pork, cheese and parsley and mix until well combined. Season to taste with salt and pepper. Pour the mixture into the loaf pan and bake for 45 minutes, or until a skewer inserted in the middle comes out clean. Remove from the oven, set on a wire rack and allow to

cool for 30 minutes before unmoulding. To unmould, run a knife around the edges, place a serving platter over the loaf pan and invert.

To serve, cut the warm cake into 1-inch slices. (Or warm it by gently pan-searing slices in a small sauté pan over medium heat with a bit of grapeseed oil and melted butter for 4 to 5 minutes per side.) Garnish with parsley and serve with the tomato jam.

Pasta dough
½ lb semolina
½ cup water

Orecchiette with Clams

This simple egg-free pasta is formed into little ears (orecchiette) and served with a fresh clam sauce. Use your favourite clams in the sauce.

Pasta dough In the bowl of a stand mixer fitted with a paddle attachment, combine the semolina and water for 5 minutes, until the dough is soft enough to work but dry enough that it doesn't easily stick to itself. To test it, pinch off a bit of dough and smear it against a dry wooden cutting board. If it does not stick to the wood but adheres a bit to your hands, you've got the right texture. (If it is still too sticky, work in another 2 Tbsp of semolina.) Cover the dough with plastic wrap and allow it to rest at room temperature for at least 20 minutes or up to 12 hours.

Divide the dough into 4 equal pieces and roll each one into a sausage ½ inch in diameter. Cut the sausages into ½-inch dumplings. Place your thumb over each dumpling, and press down and away from your body, like you are flattening it on the counter. While pressing away, the dumpling should curl up behind your thumb. The pasta should look like a little ear, with a slightly thick rim (the lobe). Set aside. (Will keep frozen for several months; toss in a generous amount of either semolina or regular flour, arrange in a single layer on a baking sheet and freeze before wrapping in plastic wrap. Or simply refrigerate on a baking sheet with lots of semolina or regular flour for up to 48 hours.)

Confit grape tomatoes

1 dry pint of grape tomatoes
½ cup extra-virgin olive oil
1 garlic bulb, cloves separated
    and peeled
1 tsp kosher salt
1 fresh medium red chili,
    kept whole

Clam sauce

2 Tbsp unsalted butter
2 Tbsp chopped shallots
2 lbs littleneck clams, rinsed well
½ cup dry white wine
1 Tbsp tiny capers
fresh dill to taste
cracked black pepper to taste

Confit grape tomatoes Preheat the oven to 375°F. Place all the ingredients in an oven-proof pan, mix well to combine and cook for 15 minutes. Remove from the oven and set aside. (Will keep, covered and refrigerated, indefinitely.)

Clam sauce Melt 1 Tbsp of the butter in a medium pot over medium-low heat. Add the shallots and cook until soft, then stir in the clams. Pour in the white wine, cover and cook until all the clams are opened, 2 to 4 minutes. Using a slotted spoon, transfer the clams to a bowl. (Discard any clams that do not open.) Reserve the clam cooking liquid.

Finish the pasta Bring a large pot of salted water to a boil over high heat.

While the water is coming to a boil, reduce the clam cooking liquid by half over medium heat, 4 to 5 minutes.

Cook the pasta for about 3 minutes until al dente. Drain and place in a large bowl.

Whisk the remaining 1 Tbsp of butter into the reduced clam liquid and pour it over the pasta. Stir in the clams, then add the capers, dill and cracked black pepper and toss well.

To serve, scoop the orecchiette and clam sauce into 4 small bowls, drizzle the confit tomatoes on top *et voilà*!

Barbounya

—— *chef* ——

FISUN ERCAN

Fisun Ercan grew up in Turkey cooking with her mother and grandmother, and she's brought many of those family dishes to her diners in Montreal, first with the highly acclaimed Restaurant Su and now at Barbounya. In Turkey, a *meyhane* is a bar known for its apéritif and mezze service, and Barbounya is just such a place. Named for a small red mullet commonly found on the Aegean Coast where Fisun grew up, this popular Outremont restaurant is a perfect spot to unwind with friends or strike up a conversation with others perched on the bar stools at its dozen or so communal tables.

The menu is light Mediterranean market cuisine with Turkish flair, and the dishes are served as small, shared plates, just like in a Turkish meyhane. An accomplished chef and cookbook author, Fisun prepares elegant dishes from the sea and from the farm, such as grilled sardines, ceviche and bouillabaisse as well as duck magret, veal liver and fried quail. She also offers exquisite vegetarian fare such as this simple but flavourful barley salad and a lovely stuffed eggplant. Barbounya is a great night out for a light and healthy meal to share with a group of friends.

4 small Italian eggplants
2 cups grapeseed (or canola) oil
  for pan-frying
¼ cup extra-virgin olive oil
1 onion, thinly sliced
4 to 5 garlic cloves, peeled and
  left whole

3 to 4 tomatoes, peeled, cored
  and chopped
1 cubanelle pepper, seeded
  and sliced
sea salt and black pepper to taste
½ cup packed roughly chopped
  fresh parsley

Oil-Poached Eggplant Stuffed with Tomatoes and Caramelized Onions

Serves four

This dish can be served as a mezze, which is the traditional way, or as an accompaniment to any grilled meat or as a main dish with rice and/or crusty bread and some plain yogurt. Look for cubanelles, also known as Cuban sweet peppers, in your local grocery store, or substitute a green bell pepper.

Fill a bowl large enough to hold the eggplants with salted water. Keeping the stem on, peel the eggplants lengthwise, alternating strips of peeled and unpeeled skin all the way around each eggplant. Starting at the stem end of each eggplant, cut a lengthwise incision ½ inch deep along one side. Place the eggplants in salted water and allow to soak for 30 minutes. (This step prevents the eggplants from oxidizing (turning brown) and absorbing too much oil when cooked.) Pat dry the eggplants with a paper towel.

Line a baking sheet with paper towels. Heat the grapeseed (or canola) oil in a deep-sided sauté pan over medium-high heat. Using tongs, and keeping your face well away from the pot, lower the eggplants into the hot oil and cook each side until golden and the flesh is soft, about 3 minutes total. Transfer the eggplants to the baking sheet.

Heat the olive oil in a sauté pan over medium-high heat. Add the onions and cook until tender, about 10 minutes, then add the garlic cloves, tomatoes and cubanelle peppers and season with salt and pepper. Reduce the heat to medium, and cover and cook for 10 to 15 minutes. Season with salt and pepper to taste.

Preheat the oven to 400°F. Arrange the eggplants in a deep ovenproof tray. Using your fingers, open each eggplant along the incision line. Spoon the tomato-onion mixture generously over each eggplant, pour any pan juices on top and bake for 10 minutes. Remove from the oven, allow to cool to room temperature and serve.

1 cup pearl barley
½ small onion, peeled and cut in half
1 celery stalk, cut in half
1 small carrot, cut in half
2 garlic cloves, unpeeled
1 bay leaf
1 Tbsp sea salt
8 cups water
½ cup roughly chopped fresh parsley
½ cup thinly sliced fresh mint
½ cup roughly chopped fresh dill
½ cup very thinly sliced shallots

2 Tbsp extra-virgin olive oil
juice of 1 lemon
toasted pine nuts for garnish
goji berries softened in white
　wine for garnish

Barley Salad with Mixed Herbs, Goji Berries and Pine Nuts

Serves eight

Place the barley, onions, celery, carrots, garlic, bay leaf and salt in a large saucepan. Pour in the water and cook uncovered over medium heat for 30 minutes, or until the grains are tender but still firm. Drain well. Remove and discard the onions, celery, carrots, garlic and bay leaf. Spread the barley on a baking sheet and allow it to cool completely.

In a medium bowl, combine the parsley, mint, dill and shallots until well mixed. Spoon the barley into a large bowl, add the olive oil, lemon juice and mixed herbs and toss until the ingredients are well combined.

To serve, divide the barley salad into individual bowls, and garnish generously with toasted pine nuts and goji berries.

Bishop & Bagg

—— *chef* ——

PELOPIDAS
BRISSON-TSAVOUSSIS

Located in the heart of the Mile End, where quaint restaurants are welcomed on every block, Bishop & Bagg references its cross streets, which are named after two neighbourhood icons from the nineteenth century: Monsignor Ignace Bourget, the bishop of Montreal; and Stanley Clark Bagg, a notary, landowner and justice of the peace. This younger brother to the Burgundy Lion (page 26), the Brit-Montreal institution, is authentic English pub in its service and design yet its menu is anything but traditional.

Leading the kitchen is gentle Pelopidas Brisson-Tsavoussis, one of Montreal's most talented young chefs, whose résumé includes stints at Joe Beef, Liverpool House and Black Strap BBQ. Pelo has a knack for doing the simple very well, and we love his crab gratin on toast, which is decidedly influenced by popular seaside village pubs in the south of England. He also conjures up images of English countryside farmers' markets with the layered flavours of his maple-mustard glazed pork belly. In addition to this being a great place to dine, we are grateful to come here for a pick-me-up at the end of a long workday. The pub has an impressive selection of gins, beer, cocktails and whisky that helps build our appetite.

facing MAPLE-MUSTARD GLAZED
PORK BELLY WITH ENDIVES

Slow-roasted pork belly
2½ lbs skinless, boneless pork belly
salt and pepper
6 garlic cloves, chopped
1 sprig fresh rosemary, chopped
zest of 1 orange
4 to 6 endives
knob of butter
drop of canola or vegetable oil
¼ cup fresh parsley leaves

Macerated grapes
20 seedless red grapes
  (Concords are really the best)
1 Tbsp white sugar
1 Tbsp red wine vinegar
pinch of ground cinnamon

Maple-mustard glaze
¼ cup maple syrup
1 Tbsp Dijon mustard
1 tsp kosher salt

Maple-Mustard Glazed Pork Belly with Endives

Serves 4 to 6

To be really decadent with this dish, reserve the pan drippings once you remove the pork belly from the oven. If they are not burnt, refrigerate them until the fat separates from the jelly. Use a spoon to scoop off and discard the hard fat, then add the jelly to the maple-mustard glaze when you coat the crispy belly.

Slow-roasted pork belly Place the pork belly in a large shallow bowl and sprinkle lightly with salt and pepper. Using your hands, rub the garlic, rosemary and orange zest into the meat. Cover and refrigerate for at least 2 hours or, better, up to 12 hours.

Preheat the oven to 250°F. Line a baking sheet with parchment paper, set the pork belly on top and cook for 3 to 5 hours, until the internal temperature of the meat reaches 185°F or a small knife can be inserted with little resistance. Remove from the oven and allow to cool to room temperature.

Macerated grapes Cut the grapes in half lengthwise and place them in a bowl. Add the sugar, vinegar and cinnamon, toss to combine, cover with plastic wrap and allow to sit at room temperature for 1 hour.

Maple-mustard glaze In a small bowl, combine the maple syrup, mustard and salt and set aside.

Finish pork belly Cut the endives in half lengthwise and score the cut faces lightly in a criss-cross pattern. Place a nonstick pan over medium heat. Add a knob of butter and a drop of cooking oil to prevent the butter from burning. When the butter has melted and the foam has subsided, season the endives with salt and place them, cut sides down, in the pan. Cook until lightly browned, 4 to 6 minutes, then flip them over and cook for 4 to 6 minutes more, until translucent and softened. Remove from the heat and set aside.

Cut the pork belly into 4 equal strips. Drain the excess fat from the endive pan and return to the heat on medium-high. Add the pork belly, cut sides down, and cook until crisp and golden, 4 to 6 minutes. Turn the meat over and cook the other side, 4 to 6 minutes more. (If you are afraid of burning the meat, cook it over medium to medium-low heat instead,

for 5 to 10 minutes per side.) Turn off the heat, transfer the pork belly to a plate and drain the excess fat from the pan.

Add the maple-mustard glaze to the hot pan. Return the pork belly to the pan and roll it around until well coated with the glaze.

To serve, arrange one slice of pork belly on each plate, top with 2 seared endive halves and one-quarter or one-sixth of the grapes (without the macerating juice). Sprinkle with parsley and spoon some of the leftover pan glaze around the plate.

2 cups milk
2 garlic cloves, peeled
2 bay leaves
2 Tbsp + a knob of butter
¼ cup all-purpose flour
salt, black pepper and nutmeg
   to taste
12 to 15 button mushrooms, sliced
splash of white or blond beer
1 lb cooked crabmeat, drained
   and picked for cartilage (fresh
   cooked or frozen is better but
   canned works)

1 Tbsp whole-grain Dijon mustard
chopped fresh parsley
4 to 6 slices crusty bread, cut into
   ¾-inch slices
olive oil or melted butter for drizzling
¼ cup (or more) grated Parmesan or
   Gruyère cheese for sprinkling

Serves 4 to 6

Crab Gratin on Toast

Serve this toast on its own, with a crisp, fresh salad or topped with a fried egg for breakfast—your choice.

Make a white sauce by placing the milk, garlic and bay leaves in a small pot over medium-high heat. When the milk comes to a boil, remove from the heat and allow the flavours to infuse for 15 minutes.

In a separate saucepan, melt the 2 Tbsp of butter over medium heat. Stir in the flour, and continue to stir until fragrant and foamy, 4 to 6 minutes. This is your roux.

Remove the garlic and bay leaves from the milk and discard them. Slowly whisk the milk into the roux ¼ cup at a time, making sure it is smooth between each addition. Once all the milk has been added, bring the sauce to a boil. Reduce the heat to low and simmer, stirring frequently, for 5 minutes or until the sauce is thick. Season with salt and pepper and a little bit of nutmeg. Remove from the heat and set aside.

Melt a knob of butter in a frying pan over medium heat. Add the mushrooms and cook until they begin to release their moisture. Add a splash of beer and season with salt and pepper. Cook until most of the liquid has evaporated, 4 to 6 minutes. Add the mushrooms and their juice to the white sauce. Fold in the crabmeat, mustard and parsley and season to taste.

Turn your broiler on. Arrange the bread slices on a baking sheet and brush or drizzle them with olive oil or melted butter. Broil the bread on one side until it is dark golden brown, then turn it over to toast the other side. Keep a close eye on them so they don't burn.

Spoon the crab mixture evenly over the toast, sprinkle them generously with cheese and broil until the cheese has melted and browned. Serve immediately.

Le Bremner

— *chef* —

DANNY SMILES

Le Bremner opened to strong buzz in 2011, and this sister restaurant to Chuck Hughes's Garde Manger (page 52) is still one of the hottest spots in the city several years later. With no sign and just two red lights indicating that the restaurant is open for service, we always feel like we've discovered a secret hangout in Old Montreal when we walk down the stairs and into the nineteenth-century stone building and private courtyard terrace.

We like to bring out-of-town guests here for the warm and friendly service, the inventive drinks and humorous banter at the bar and the playful seafood cuisine captained by Chef Danny Smiles.

Chef Smiles started in the dish pit of his parents' small hotel restaurant in Montreal, did a couple of *stages* with Michelin-starred chefs in Brescia and Soverato, Italy, and distinguished himself as the runner-up on the third season of *Top Chef Canada*. He's as much at home in the dining room as the kitchen, where he and his team whip up exceptional crudo dishes and our favourite, salmon beet gravlax. Le Bremner may be hard to find, but we find it even harder to leave!

facing SALMON BEET GRAVLAX

Salmon beet gravlax

½ side of salmon, skin on, 1 to 1½ lbs, pin bones removed
¼ cup kosher salt
¼ cup white sugar
juice of 3 red beets (or grate 3 beets on a box grater)
3 fl oz vodka
¼ cup freshly grated horseradish
1 shallot, finely chopped
1 fresh bird's-eye chili, finely chopped
¼ cup fresh lime juice
1 cup frisée lettuce for garnish
extra-virgin olive oil for drizzling

Roasted garlic

1 garlic bulb, unpeeled
olive oil
salt and pepper

Dill sour cream

1 cup sour cream
1 clove roasted garlic (recipe here), peeled
¼ cup finely chopped fresh dill
1 Tbsp white balsamic vinegar
salt and pepper

Serves eight

Salmon Beet Gravlax

Start this dish at least two days before you plan to serve it so the salmon has time to cure. And roast the garlic ahead of time. Then, once the fish is ready, the rest of the dish comes together quickly.

Salmon beet gravlax With paper towels, pat dry the salmon. Using your hands, massage the salt into the salmon and place it in a large, shallow pan. Cover with the sugar and then pour the beet juice (or grated beets) and vodka overtop. Coat with the grated horseradish. Cover the pan with plastic wrap and refrigerate for 48 hours.

Roasted garlic Preheat the oven to 275°F. Have ready a square of aluminum foil.

Using a sharp knife, cut the tops off the garlic, exposing the top of the cloves. Place the garlic on the foil. Drizzle generously with olive oil and sprinkle with salt and pepper. Wrap the garlic tightly in the foil and roast for 2 hours. Remove from the oven and set aside.

Dill sour cream Place all of the ingredients in a blender and blend until smooth. Scoop into a small serving bowl and set aside.

Fried capers
1 cup canola or vegetable oil
    for deep-frying
½ cup capers

Fried capers Line a plate with paper towels. Fill a small, deep-sided pot with the canola (or vegetable) oil, and heat over medium-high heat until it reaches 350°F. (Use a deep-fry thermometer to test the temperature.) Very carefully add the capers, keeping your face away from the pot, and cook for about 30 seconds, or until they have burst open and become crispy. Using a slotted spoon, scoop the capers from the pot and allow them to drain on the paper towel–lined plate. Set aside.

Finish gravlax Remove the salmon from the fridge, rinse under cold running water and dry with paper towels. Using a very sharp knife, remove and discard the salmon skin. Cut the salmon in half lengthwise, then slice it very thinly and arrange the slices in a single layer on individual plates. Sprinkle with salt and pepper, shallots and chilies. Squeeze lime juice over each portion. Garnish with capers and leaves of frisée lettuce. Lightly drizzle extra-virgin olive oil around the plate, and serve the dill sour cream on the side.

3 cups whole milk
½ cup plain white vinegar
4 cups all-purpose flour
4 Tbsp baking powder
2 Tbsp baking soda
½ cup white sugar
pinch of salt
4 large eggs

½ Tbsp vanilla extract
½ cup melted butter for the
   batter + 2 to 4 Tbsp butter
   to grease the pan
½ cup unsalted butter, room
   temperature, for whipping
dark amber maple syrup for
   pouring

Bremner Pancakes with Whipped Butter and Maple Syrup

Serves 4 to 6 (makes twelve 5-inch pancakes)

This dessert has become a staple in the Bremner repertoire. These light, fluffy pancakes are easy to make and can be enjoyed at breakfast, at lunch or as a sweet finish to dinner. This will surely become your go-to pancake recipe.

Combine the milk and vinegar in a large bowl, cover and allow to sit at room temperature for 30 minutes.

In another large bowl, sift together the flour, baking powder and baking soda. Stir in the sugar and salt.

In a third bowl, whisk together the eggs and vanilla, and then stir them into the milk mixture.

Add the dry ingredients to the milk mixture in 3 parts, stirring after each addition just until you see no more dry bits. Be careful not to overmix. Stir in the melted butter.

Preheat a large nonstick frying pan over medium heat. When the pan is hot, add 2 Tbsp of the butter and allow it to melt. Cook 3 pancakes at a time, ladling about ⅓ cup batter per pancake into the pan and tilting the pan to get a circle about 5 inches in diameter. Cook until golden, about 4 minutes, then flip the pancakes over to cook the other side. Transfer the cooked pancakes to a plate. Repeat with the remaining batter. (You should have 12 pancakes.)

While the pancakes are cooking, place the room temperature butter in the bowl of a stand mixer fitted with a whisk attachment. Whip the butter at high speed until it becomes light and doubles in size, about 6 minutes. Scrape the butter into a small bowl and set aside.

To serve, place 2 to 3 pancakes on individual plates. Serve with a scoop of whipped butter and a generous splash of maple syrup.

Burgundy Lion

—— *chef* ——

TOBY LYLE,
PAUL DESBAILLETS,
WILL ALLEN AND
JEAN-MICHEL CREUSOT

Little Burgundy in Montreal was a very quiet part of the city until 2008 when four old friends, all from the restaurant and bar industry, took over an old building and created two floors of boisterous cheer fuelled by an extensive beer selection, over 400 varieties of whisky and a unique Brit-Quebecois menu. The Burgundy Lion is a laid-back British pub where soccer fans gather at the long wooden bar to cheer on their favourite teams, where the walls are covered in British memorabilia and where we like to kick back with a London Tea Party and classic mains like fish 'n' chips and bangers and mash.

While this is a great place to get a taste of Old Blighty, the Burgundy Lion is also a good spot to have fun and meet new people. Its signature crest—which represents the pub's famous lion; a royal crown; and Montreal's coat of arms referencing the English, the Scots, the Irish and the French—and its motto, *Ubi bene ibi patria* ("Where you feel good, there is your home"), capture exactly how we feel here. The Burgundy Lion never disappoints.

⅓ cup mayonnaise
½ tsp Madras curry powder
4 cans (each 6 oz) tuna
2 green onions, thinly sliced
salt and pepper
2 Tbsp salted butter, room
    temperature
8 slices white bread
½ English cucumber, sliced
    in thin rounds
8 slices brown bread

Serves four

London Tea Party

Afternoon tea is popular in Britain, and dainty sandwiches with the crusts cut off are a popular accompaniment. Here are two classic variations fit for a pub and your lunch table.

In a small bowl, combine the mayonnaise and curry powder until well mixed. Cover and refrigerate until needed.

Drain the tuna well and place it in a medium bowl. Stir in the green onions and curry mayonnaise and season to taste with salt and pepper. Set aside.

Butter one side of 4 slices of the white bread. Top each slice with 6 to 8 pieces of cucumber and season with salt and pepper. Cover the cucumber with a second slice of white bread.

Spread one-quarter of the tuna mixture on one side of 4 slices of brown bread. Spread the tuna evenly to the edge of the bread. Season lightly with salt and pepper, and top the tuna with another slice of brown bread.

Stack 2 tuna sandwiches on top of each other, making sure the corners are aligned. Using a sharp knife, cut off the crusts all the way around the bread. Discard the crusts. Repeat with the other 2 sandwiches. Cut the sandwiches corner to corner to create 4 triangles per stack. Repeat the stacking and cutting with the cucumber sandwiches.

To serve, arrange the sandwiches on a serving platter, alternating tuna with cucumber. Serve immediately.

16 cups canola oil for deep-frying
1 cup all-purpose flour
1 cup panko bread crumbs
1¼ cups cornstarch
¾ tsp baking powder
2 tsp Cajun spice
2 tsp kosher salt

2 tsp black pepper
1 cup soda water
1½ cups beer, preferably ale
  (about 1 bottle)
6 skinless, boneless cod fillets,
  each 5 to 6 oz
1 lemon, cut into wedges (optional)

Fish 'n' Chips

Serves 4 to 6

This battered fish dish is perfect served with your favourite fries, mushy peas and ketchup and tartar sauce. If you don't have a deep fryer, cook them up in a large, deep, heavy-bottomed pot.

Preheat a deep fryer to 350°F, or fill a large, deep-sided pot with the canola oil and heat it over medium-high until the temperature reaches 350°F, using a deep-fry thermometer to check the temperature. Line a large plate with paper towels.

In a large, shallow bowl, mix together the flour, panko, cornstarch, baking powder, Cajun spice and salt and pepper until well combined. Slowly add the soda water, whisking constantly, so the batter doesn't form lumps. Add the beer, a bit at a time, until the batter has the consistency of pancake batter. Reserve ¼ cup of the beer in case you need to fix the batter later.

Using a clean tea towel, gently pat dry the cod fillets. Season the fish with salt and pepper.

Dip the fillets in the batter, ensuring they are well coated. Using tongs, carefully lower the fish, 2 pieces at a time, into the hot oil, and allow it to cook for 5 to 6 minutes, or until golden. Transfer the fillets to the paper towel–lined plate, then cut into one of them with a sharp knife to ensure they are cooked. The flesh should flake easily. Repeat with the remaining fish fillets. Serve immediately, with wedges of lemon.

Chez Sophie

— *chef* —

SOPHIE TABET

Born in Lebanon and partly raised in Montreal, Sophie Tabet prepares unpretentious but pure and elegant meals at her eponymous Chez Sophie in Griffintown. From the moment we step in the door, there's an air of serenity and tranquility wafting through the dining room. Decorated in cream and light grey, the room has seats at the bar and at twelve tables, each adorned with delicate porcelain sculpture and custom-made dinnerware created by Lebanese artists. What most stands out, however, is Sophie's colourful, flavourful food.

A graduate of the Institut Paul Bocuse near Lyon, Sophie worked in Michelin-starred restaurants in France and Italy—where she met her sommelier husband, Marco Marangi—and in her family's eatery in Lebanon. In 2013, she and Marco returned to Montreal to open Chez Sophie, which is deservedly known for its bright, clean French cuisine with touches of Italian flavours and hints of unique spices. Sophie does not follow trends, and so we can always rely on her for food that highlights its components. We especially love her table d'hôte lunch menu that changes daily: like the restaurant itself, these are classy dishes that will never go out of style.

½ cup sake
½ cup mirin
6 Tbsp white sugar
1 cup white miso paste
¼ cup yuzu juice
4 black cod (sablefish) fillets,
    skin on, each 6 to 7 oz

Black Cod
Glazed with Miso

Serves four

This dish comes together very quickly once the black cod has been marinated, but allow twenty-four hours to marinate the fish. Yuzu juice (a citrus fruit and plant originating in East Asia) and mirin (sweet cooking wine) are available at Asian grocery stores, sake (rice wine) at the SAQ or your local fully stocked liquor store. If you can't find yuzu, buy lemon grass instead, cut it into pieces and boil it with the sake and mirin. Serve the fish with grilled or wok-fried vegetables.

Bring the sake and mirin to a boil in a medium saucepan over high heat. Allow to boil for 20 seconds to evaporate the alcohol. Reduce the heat to low and stir in the sugar until it dissolves. Remove from the heat, add the miso paste and whisk until well combined. Allow the marinade to cool to room temperature, about 30 minutes.

Place the cod fillets on a large plate. Using a spoon, slather the fish with the marinade until it is covered with the sauce. Set aside the remaining marinade.

Position the oven rack in the middle of the oven. Preheat the oven to 475°F. Line a baking sheet with parchment paper.

Using paper towels, gently wipe off any excess miso clinging to the fish (do not rinse the fillets), and place the fish, skin side up, on the baking sheet. Cook for about 8 minutes, until the flesh is opaque and firm to the touch. Remove the fish from the oven and turn on the broiler.

Carefully peel the skin from the fish and discard it. Gently turn the fish over, and carefully remove and discard any bones. Using a pastry brush, gently baste the fish with the remaining marinade. Broil for 4 to 5 minutes until the marinade has lightly caramelized. Serve immediately.

French toast

4 slices brioche bread,
   each 1 inch thick
4 tsp dark chocolate
   (70%–75% cocoa)
1 cup whole milk
1 cup whipping cream
¼ cup + ⅓ cup white sugar
2 large egg yolks
⅓ cup butter

Caramel

¼ cup white sugar
1 Tbsp water
¾ cup whipping cream
2 Tbsp unsalted butter
½ tsp fine sea salt

Serves four

Sophie's French Toast

French toast is often served as a decadent brunch dish, but this version is more like a dessert. It's especially delicious served warm with a scoop of vanilla ice cream. To save time, make the caramel while the bread is soaking.

French toast Using a sharp knife, make a small incision into each slice of brioche from the outer edge. Insert 1 tsp of chocolate into the middle of the bread. Arrange the bread in a single layer in a rectangular baking dish.

In a large bowl, whisk together the milk, cream, ¼ cup of sugar and egg yolks until well combined. Pour the mixture over the brioche slices and allow to soak for 20 minutes.

Caramel Combine the ¼ cup sugar and water in a small pot over high heat. Without stirring, allow the mixture to come to a boil, and continue cooking it until the sugar becomes deep amber/caramel, about 4 minutes. Remove from the heat, pour in the cream and butter and stir quickly until the butter has melted and the mixture has emulsified.

Add the salt, stir and return to the stove over medium heat. Bring the mixture to a simmer and allow it to cook for 5 minutes, or until slightly thickened. Remove from the heat and allow to cool.

Finish French toast Preheat a large sauté pan over medium heat. Add the butter and ⅓ cup of sugar and stir until melted. Place the soaked brioche slices in the pan, in batches if necessary, and cook until lightly browned, 3 to 4 minutes per side.

To serve, place a piece of French toast on each plate and spoon the warm caramel sauce overtop. Serve immediately.

Dinette Triple Crown

—— *chef* ——

COLIN PERRY

Chef Colin Perry grew up just down the hill from his grandparents in the small coal-mining town of Whitley City, Kentucky. Throughout his childhood and early adulthood, he learned from them how to cure, can and cellar whatever was in season in order to preserve it for the harsher months. Today, those rich Southern Appalachian techniques meet Eastern Canada's seasonal bounty at Rosemont's Dinette Triple Crown in well-crafted dishes.

In the spring and summer months, we opt to dine outdoors. Packed into elegant picnic baskets are a tablecloth, glass mason jars of homemade drinks, mini squeeze-bottles of sauce for our fried chicken or crispy Nashville hot pig's ears (a play on a popular fried chicken dish in Nashville that's not for the faint of heart). The menu is packed with goodness and lots of side dishes to pair with our Southern proteins. Colin and co-owner Nicole Turcotte have built a steady following, and whether we eat in the Dinette dining room, or take our picnic to the park down the street or to the table in our house, we certainly get a taste of the South.

Pig's ears

16 cups water (or more)
1 cup fine sea salt
½ cup packed brown sugar
¼ cup dried chili flakes
4 bay leaves
8 sprigs fresh thyme
1 Tbsp insta-cure #1 (optional)

8 large (or 12 small) pig's ears,
    cleaned well and any hairs removed
about 16 cups lard (rendered pork fat)
4 to 6 cups peanut oil (or vegetable,
    grapeseed or any other oil with a
    high smoke point) or enough for
    deep-frying

*Serves
4 to 6*

Nashville Hot Pig's Ears

Hot fried chicken is an institution in Nashville. Restaurants like Prince's and Bolton's have been serving this fried chicken—tossed in a delicious hot paste—to legions of devoted fans for years. We serve our version of this paste with fried pig's ears because the crispy texture just begs for some heat. These are extremely spicy as is, but if you want something closer to what gets served in Nashville, then replace all the paprika in the spice paste with more cayenne. Insta-cure #1 is a pink salt used for curing, and it has a bacony-ham flavour; find it mainly online. And start this dish three to four days before you plan to serve it, so the pig's ears have time to brine.

Pig's ears Place 8 cups of the water in a large saucepan over high heat. Add the sea salt, brown sugar, chili flakes, bay leaves and thyme and bring to a boil. Reduce the heat to low and allow to simmer for 1 hour.

Place a fine-mesh sieve over a container large enough to hold the pig's ears. Strain the brine through the sieve and discard the solids. Pour in the curing salt and stir to dissolve. Add enough cold water to make 16 cups of brine. Refrigerate until cold, about 4 hours or overnight. Once cold, add the pig's ears, placing a plate on top to keep them submerged. Allow to brine, refrigerated, for 3 days.

Preheat your oven to 200°F. Fill a large Dutch oven about half full with lard. Place the Dutch oven on the stove over medium-high heat and allow the lard to melt completely. Add the pig's ears and more lard, if necessary, to cover. When the lard is hot and the pig's ears are starting to simmer and sizzle, cover and cook in the oven until very tender, 5 to 6 hours. Remove from the oven, and allow to cool in the fat.

Bread and butter pickles

3⅓ cups large pickling cucumbers, sliced ¼ inch thick
½ cup white onions, sliced ⅛ inch thick
1 tsp pickling spice
1 cup plain white vinegar
1 cup water
½ cup white sugar
1 tsp fine sea salt
½ tsp turmeric

Buttermilk bread

3 cups all-purpose flour
2 Tbsp + 1 tsp white sugar
1 tsp instant yeast
1¼ cups buttermilk
1 large egg
1¼ Tbsp fine sea salt
3 Tbsp lard or butter, room temperature

Hot paste

1 cup lard
½ cup cayenne pepper
2 Tbsp sweet paprika
2 Tbsp smoked paprika
¼ cup garlic powder
2 Tbsp fine sea salt

Line a large baking sheet with parchment paper. Once the pig's ears have cooled, arrange them in a single layer on the baking sheet. Cover with another sheet of parchment paper and a second baking sheet. Set some heavy tins on top to press them, and refrigerate for 12 to 24 hours.

Bread and butter pickles Wash a 1-qt mason jar with a sealable lid in very hot water. Dry it well and pack the cucumbers, onions and pickling spice into the jar.

Place the vinegar, water, sugar, salt and turmeric into a medium saucepan and bring to a boil over high heat. Pour this hot pickling liquid over the vegetables, seal the jar tightly and refrigerate for at least 1 day (preferably 3) to cure. Will keep refrigerated for up to 1 month.

Buttermilk bread In the bowl of a stand mixer fitted with a paddle attachment, combine 1½ cups of the flour, the sugar, yeast, buttermilk and egg for 5 minutes on high speed. Allow the mixture to rest for 20 minutes.

Replace the paddle attachment with the dough hook. Add the remaining 1½ cups flour and the salt to the dough and mix on low speed for 5 minutes. Add the lard (or butter), and mix on low speed for another 5 to 10 minutes until the dough is smooth and elastic.

Transfer the dough to a clean bowl, cover with plastic wrap and allow to rise in a warm place until doubled in size, 1 to 2 hours.

recipe continued overleaf...

Using a paper towel, grease a 2-lb Pullman loaf pan with lard. Shape your loaf, place it in the pan and drape with a tea towel, allowing it to rise again until it is within ½ inch of the top, about 1 hour.

Preheat the oven to 350°F. Cover the loaf pan and bake for 30 minutes. Remove from the oven and turn out onto a cooling rack.

Hot paste Heat the lard in a pot over medium heat. Once hot, stir in the cayenne, sweet and smoked paprikas, garlic powder and salt, and allow the mixture to sizzle for about 30 seconds. It will become very aromatic. Transfer the mixture to a heatproof container and allow to cool. Will keep refrigerated in an airtight container for up to 1 month.

Finish pig's ears Cut 4 to 6 slices of buttermilk bread, each ½ inch thick, and place a slice on each individual plate. Half-fill a Dutch oven with peanut oil (or any other oil with a high smoke point) and heat over medium-high heat, adjusting the heat as necessary to maintain a temperature of 350°F. Using tongs and standing with your face away from the pot, place 4 pig's ears into the oil and fry for 3 to 4 minutes until crispy but not dried out. Transfer the cooked pig's ears to a bowl, and repeat with the remaining meat.

Add enough of the paste to evenly coat the pig's ears and toss well. Pile 2 to 3 pig's ears on each slice of bread, along with some of the paste from the bowl. Top with bread and butter pickles.

Chow chow

½ head regular green cabbage, cored and cut in large dice

1 small white onion, peeled and cut into 8 pieces

1 green bell pepper, cored and quartered

4 tsp fine sea salt

2 cups cider vinegar

1 cup packed light brown sugar

4 tsp yellow mustard seeds

1 tsp hot mustard powder, like Keen's

1 tsp ground ginger

1 tsp celery seeds

½ tsp turmeric

½ tsp dried chili flakes

Pinto beans

1½ cups diced good-quality slab bacon (bought from a good butcher shop)

1 Tbsp dried oregano

1 tsp dried chili flakes

2 cups finely diced onions (about 2 medium)

1 cup finely diced celery (about 2 stalks)

1 cup finely diced green bell peppers (about 1 large)

2 garlic cloves, minced

1 cup white wine

8 sprigs fresh thyme

3 cups dried pinto beans, soaked overnight and rinsed well

4 to 6 cups chicken stock

2 tsp freshly cracked black pepper

salt to taste

1 bunch green onions, white and green parts thinly sliced, for garnish

Cornbread, Pinto Beans and Chow Chow

Serves 8 to 10

This is my death-row meal. As a child in Kentucky, I recall eating it every Sunday and continue to make this variation on my mother's recipe to honour that tradition. Chow Chow is a pickled relish or chutney that originated in the Southern United States. It's commonly made with end-of-season vegetables like cabbage, peppers, green tomatoes and chayote to preserve the harvest for the winter.

Chow chow Place the cabbage, onion and bell pepper in the bowl of a food processor, and pulse until they have the consistency of green relish. Scrape the vegetables into a large bowl and sprinkle them with the salt. Toss with your hands to evenly distribute the salt. Cover and allow to sit at room temperature between 12 and 24 hours.

Drain the vegetables in a colander, then run water over them to rinse out the salt. Using your hands, gently squeeze out any excess water and set aside.

Place the vinegar, brown sugar, mustard seeds, mustard powder, ginger, celery seeds, turmeric and chili flakes in a large, heavy-bottomed pot, and bring to a simmer over high heat. Once the sugar has dissolved, stir in the vegetables and bring back to a simmer. Reduce the heat to medium and cook for 45 minutes to 1 hour, or until the vegetables are tender and the cabbage looks translucent. Remove from the heat and allow to cool. Will keep refrigerated in an airtight container for 1 month . . . or longer.

Pinto beans Place a large, heavy-bottomed pot over medium-high heat. Add the bacon and cook for 5 to 7 minutes, or until most of the fat has rendered. Pour off the excess bacon fat and reserve for the cornbread; keep the bacon in the pot.

Return the pot to the heat, stir in the oregano and chili flakes and cook for 30 seconds. Add the onions, reduce heat to medium and cook for about 5 minutes,

Cornbread

1 cup fine white cornmeal,
   preferably organic

¾ tsp fine sea salt

1 tsp baking powder

⅛ tsp baking soda

1 cup buttermilk

1 large egg

¼ cup + 2 Tbsp bacon fat, melted
   and cooled (reserved from the
   pinto bean recipe)

or until most of the water has evaporated and they become dry. Stir in the celery and bell peppers and continue cooking for 20 to 25 minutes, stirring occasionally, until the mixture has released all its water and has become dry and paste-like.

Preheat the oven to 300°F. Add the garlic to the cooked vegetables and cook for 30 more seconds. Pour in the wine and allow to simmer and reduce until mostly evaporated, about 2 minutes. Stir in the thyme and the beans, and add enough chicken stock to cover by 1 inch. Allow the mixture to come to a simmer, then use a spoon to skim any impurities that have risen to the top. Cover and bake for 1 hour. If the beans are very soft but not mushy, remove them from the oven. If they are not soft, check them every 10 to 20 minutes for another 30 minutes to 1 hour. Remove from the oven and season with plenty of pepper and salt to taste.

Cornbread Preheat the oven to 450°F. Have ready an 8-inch cast-iron frying pan.

Place the cornmeal, salt, baking powder and baking soda in a large bowl and stir until well combined. Set aside.

In a small bowl, whisk together the buttermilk and egg, then pour these wet ingredients into the cornmeal mixture. Gently stir together with a wooden spoon until fairly smooth. Add the ¼ cup of reserved bacon fat and stir to combine.

Place the frying pan over high heat. When hot, add the 2 Tbsp bacon fat, allow it to melt and then swirl it around the pan to coat well. When the pan is very hot, pour in the cornbread batter and reduce the heat to medium-high. Allow the corn-bread to "fry" in the skillet until the sides begin to firm up and the edges can easily be pulled away from the side of the pan, about 2 minutes. Transfer to the oven and bake for 10 to 15 minutes, or until a wooden skewer inserted in the middle comes out clean. Remove from the oven and slide the cornbread out of the pan and onto a cooling rack.

To serve Spoon some of the beans into each bowl. Top with a large spoonful of chow chow and a generous sprinkle of green onions. Serve with cornbread on the side and plenty of your favourite hot sauce.

Dominion
Square Tavern

—— chef ——

ERIC DUPUIS

Situated in the heart of the Golden Square Mile in downtown Montreal, the Dominion Square Tavern first opened as a hotel-restaurant in the Roaring Twenties. The hotel was later ravaged by fire, leaving behind only the restaurant, and the building was reincarnated in the 1970s as one of the city's first gay bars. Patrons entered discreetly by the back alley, where the original sign still hangs. Women were barred until 1988 when a new law revoked the men's-only access to taverns across Quebec. By 2009 when Eric Dupuis stepped in as chef, Dominion Square Tavern had returned to its restaurant roots.

On the menu are bistro-style dishes with a nod to Eric's French-Canadian heritage and to British cuisine. There is *pâté de campagne*, the traditional French rustic pork terrine, as well as a Scotch egg with hints of ginger, coriander, cumin and caraway that reference India's influence on British food. Similarly, there are French fries served with mayonnaise as well as traditional British desserts such as a sticky toffee pudding. This is impeccably prepared food that inspires comfort without pretense, all served in a smart and storied room.

Sausage-wrapped eggs
¾ lb pork shoulder, cut
  into cubes
4 fresh sage leaves, chopped
1 garlic clove, minced
1 Tbsp chopped fresh ginger
½ tsp ground cumin
¼ tsp ground caraway
¼ tsp ground coriander

¼ tsp cayenne pepper
½ tsp kosher salt
7 large eggs
1 cup all-purpose flour
1 cup dried bread crumbs
4 cups canola oil for
  deep-frying
sprigs of watercress
  for garnish

Swedish sauce
1 cup mayonnaise
  (homemade is best)
¼ cup applesauce
1 tsp prepared horseradish

Serves four

Scotch Eggs

Scotch eggs are not actually from Scotland but from Great Britain. They were invented by the Fortnum & Mason department store in 1738. Serve them with a fresh green salad.

Sausage-wrapped eggs In a large bowl, mix the pork, sage, garlic, ginger, cumin, caraway, coriander, cayenne and salt until well combined. Cover and refrigerate for 12 hours.

Using a meat grinder fitted with a ⅛-inch plate, grind the meat. Cover and refrigerate it while you prepare the eggs and breading.

Fill a large bowl with ice water. Bring a large pot of water to a boil over high heat. Drop 4 eggs into the boiling water and cook them for 5 minutes. Transfer the eggs to the ice water and allow them to cool. Once they are cold, peel them carefully. Discard the shells and set aside the boiled eggs.

Divide the sausage meat into 4 equal portions. Using your hands, press the sausage meat around each soft-boiled egg, completely encasing it.

Pour the flour onto a large, shallow plate and the bread crumbs into a wide bowl.

Crack the remaining 3 eggs into a small bowl and whisk them well. Gently roll each of the sausage-wrapped eggs in the flour, then in the eggs and finally in the bread crumbs. Refrigerate the eggs while you make the sauce.

Swedish sauce Mix together all of the ingredients until well combined.

Finish sausage-wrapped eggs Preheat the oven to 400°F and a deep fryer to 350°F. (If you do not have a deep fryer, fill a deep-sided pot with canola oil and heat it over medium-high heat until it reaches 350°F. Use a deep-fry thermometer to test the temperature.)

Using tongs or a fryer basket, carefully place the sausage-wrapped eggs into the hot oil and cook for 2 minutes. Transfer to a baking sheet and cook in the oven for 5 minutes.

To serve, spread some Swedish sauce in the middle of 4 individual plates, top with watercress and arrange an egg on top. Serve immediately.

Beer-braised beef

2 lbs beef blade pot roast,
    trimmed of fat
salt and pepper
2 Tbsp sunflower oil
2 carrots, roughly chopped
1 onion, roughly chopped
1 garlic bulb, cloves separated
    and peeled

1 leek, roughly chopped
4 sprigs fresh thyme
3 bay leaves
3 cups stout beer
1 cup canned tomatoes
8 cups good-quality veal stock
¼ cup fancy molasses

Mashed potatoes

4 Yukon Gold potatoes, peeled
    and cut into pieces
6 garlic cloves, peeled
salt and pepper
½ cup unsalted butter
1 cup whipping cream
2 cups grated old cheddar

Serves four

Stout Beer–Braised Beef

This classic dish is popular at the Dominion Square Tavern. We use a fresh sunflower oil called Volte-Face (Les Cèdres) from Société-Orignal in our carrot salad. If you're not able to find this particular brand, use any high-quality sunflower oil instead.

Beer-braised beef Preheat the oven to 350°F. Season the beef with salt and pepper. Heat the sunflower oil in a large ovenproof Dutch oven or heavy-bottomed pot over medium-high heat. Add the beef and sear on all sides until well caramelized, about 6 minutes. Using a slotted spoon, transfer the meat to a plate.

Add the carrots, onions, garlic and leeks to the casserole and cook until softened, about 5 minutes. Stir in the thyme, bay leaves and beer and cook until reduced by half, about 3 minutes. Pour in the tomatoes, veal stock and molasses and bring to a boil. Return the beef to the pot, cover the pot, slide it into the oven and cook for 4 hours, basting the meat every 15 minutes and removing the lid after 2 hours. The meat should be tender and easily pull from the bone.

Mashed potatoes Place the potatoes and garlic in a large pot and cover with salted water. Bring the water to a boil over high heat, then reduce the heat to low and cook until the potatoes are soft, 10 to 15 minutes.

Carrot salad
3 carrots, thinly sliced on a mandolin
1 Tbsp prepared horseradish
2 tsp high-quality fresh sunflower oil
1 cup fresh flat-leaf parsley leaves
salt and pepper

While the potatoes are cooking, place the butter and cream in a small pot over low heat and cook, stirring, until the butter has melted.

Drain the potatoes in a colander, then run them through a ricer (or mash them) to get smooth, mashed flesh. Place the potatoes, cheese and the cream mixture in a large saucepan over high heat. Stir continuously until the mixture makes big bubbles. Season to taste with salt and pepper.

Carrot salad Fill a large bowl with ice water. Bring a medium pot of salted water to a boil over high heat. Add the carrots and blanch for 1 minute. Drain the carrots and place them in the ice water to stop the cooking. Drain the carrots again and pat them dry with paper towels.

In a serving bowl, toss together the carrots, horseradish, sunflower oil and parsley. Season to taste with salt and pepper.

To serve Spoon a generous dollop of mashed potatoes into the centre of 4 warm, deep plates. Arrange a piece of the beef on top. Strain the beef jus through a fine-mesh sieve into a measuring cup. Discard the solids. Pour some of the jus over the beef, and finish the plate with some carrot salad on top of the meat.

Ferreira Café

—— *chef* ——

JOÃO DIAS

On Peel Street in the heart of downtown Montreal is the vibrant Ferreira Café, a cornerstone of the restaurant scene since 1996. On any given day, diners include a veritable who's who of the city's business world, as men and women in suits close deals over plates of Chef João Dias's authentic and modern Portuguese cuisine. We like Ferreira Café because, especially on a cold or snowy Montreal day, it's like stepping into the sunny Mediterranean.

Owner Carlos Ferreira and his family have worked hard to create an inviting space and memorable food, and that success has led to Vasco da Gama, a takeout café, and Taverne F, which offers shared plates (*petiscos*) in the entertainment district. But Ferreira Café is still the place we go to enjoy creative twists on time-honoured traditional dishes—such as seafood bouillabaisse and Lagareiro-style grilled octopus made with fish and other ingredients freshly arrived from Portugal. Since taking over the kitchen in 2013, João Dias has brought his own touch to the menu. Trained in Portugal, he apprenticed in Spain with three-star Michelin chef Martín Berasategui and travelled to Brazil and the United States before landing in Montreal to woo us with new interpretations of various regional dishes. *Bom apetite!*

1 white onion, cut into thin strips

2 garlic cloves, minced

2 red heirloom tomatoes, cut into thin strips

3 mini bell peppers (ideally red, yellow and green for some colour), cut into thin strips

8 fingerling potatoes, thinly sliced

1 fresh squid (usually about 6 oz), cleaned and cut into thin rings

4 mussels with shell, rinsed well under cold water

4 razor clams with shell, rinsed well under cold water (or 4 regular clams or mussels)

4 clams with shell, rinsed well under cold water

1 octopus tentacle (usually about 10 oz), rinsed well and then boiled until tender, usually about 45 minutes

4 raw Matane shrimp with shell

sea salt and black pepper

1 bay leaf

1 tsp piri-piri sauce (or another hot sauce)

1 tsp curry powder

¼ cup olive oil

½ cup white wine

1 small bunch fresh parsley + some finely chopped for garnish

1 small bunch fresh cilantro + some finely chopped for garnish

1 small bunch fresh mint + some finely chopped for garnish

Cataplana de Marisco
(Seafood Bouillabaisse)

Serves four

This stew is a very traditional dish made in Portugal using seafood and sometimes fresh fish. It is cooked traditionally in a cataplana, a rounded copper or stainless steel pot with a hinged lid. However, if you do not have one, a regular casserole will make it just as delicious.

Arrange the vegetables in layers in the cataplana or a pot, starting with the onions and garlic, then the tomatoes, bell peppers and potatoes. Top with layers of the squid, the mussels, razor clams and regular clams, and the octopus. End with the shrimp. Season with sea salt and pepper, then add the bay leaf, and sprinkle with the piri-piri sauce and the curry powder. Pour in the olive oil and the white wine. Set the bunches of parsley, cilantro and mint on top. Cover and cook over medium-low heat for 20 to 25 minutes, or until the vegetables are tender. Adjust the seasoning with salt and pepper, and a little piri-piri if you like it spicier. Garnish with minced fresh herbs. Bring the cataplana to the table and serve family-style.

Caesar dressing

2 oil-packed anchovies
1 tsp Worcestershire sauce
1 large soft-boiled egg, peeled
zest and juice of 1 lime
1 tsp piri-piri sauce
    (or another hot sauce)
1 tsp red wine vinegar
1 tsp minced garlic
2 Tbsp chopped fresh cilantro
¾ cup olive oil

Croutons

8 paper-thin slices of cornbread
    (or another bread)
¼ cup olive oil
¾ oz dry chorizo sausage, cut
    into small cubes (to infuse
    flavour into the croutons)
1 tsp smoked paprika

Caesar salad

2 fresh sea urchins (optional)
4 baby romaine lettuce, washed,
    dried and separated into leaves
2 Tbsp olive oil
¼ cup white wine vinegar
    sea salt and black pepper
1 to 1¼ lbs lobster, boiled or steamed
    and cut into ¼-inch slices
8 Matane shrimp, cooked
¼ cup Caesar dressing (recipe here)
    pinch of ground Espelette pepper
    red sorrel micro greens and
    amaranth sprouts and flowers,
    for garnish (optional)

Serves 4 as an appetizer

Ferreira Caesar Salad

Piri-piri is a Portuguese hot pepper sauce, and Espelette pepper is a French chili pepper, which is sold dried and ground. Both can be found in many supermarkets and specialty food shops.

Caesar dressing Place all of the ingredients, except the olive oil, in a blender and combine until well mixed. With the motor running, slowly pour in the olive oil until the dressing emulsifies and has the consistency of mayonnaise. Will keep refrigerated in an airtight container for up to 3 days.

Croutons Preheat the oven to 350°F. Place the bread slices in a single layer on a baking sheet, dress with the olive oil, sprinkle with chorizo cubes and paprika and bake until golden, about 5 minutes. Shake off the cubes of chorizo and set aside.

Caesar salad Prepare the urchin, if using. Have ready a tea towel and a pair of sharp kitchen scissors. Using the tea towel, pick up one of the urchins with one hand. With the scissors, snip around the top of the spiky shell to make an opening. Pour off and discard any liquid and continue to cut off the top of the shell to expose the flesh beneath. Carefully release the orange meat from the shell and set aside. Discard the shell. Repeat with the second sea urchin.

Place the lettuce in a large bowl, add the olive oil, white wine vinegar and sea salt and toss until the leaves are well coated. Top the crisp romaine with the sliced lobster, the shrimp and the sea urchin. Gently spoon the Caesar dressing around the seafood. Sprinkle the salad with a pinch of Espelette pepper and season it with a little sea salt and pepper. Garnish with the croutons and the sprouts and fresh flowers. Serve immediately.

Garde Manger

—— *chef* ——

JOSH LAURIDSEN

Early in the evening, Garde Manger is the place that professionals come to have a quiet dinner. Later, bouncing crowds order drinks on a tab and feast on rows of seafood platters that flow steadily from the kitchen. Chef Chuck Hughes opened this popular Old Montreal restaurant in 2006, and it has quickly become one of the pre-eminent destination restaurants in this city—due, no doubt, to the exquisite menu and Chuck's down-to-earth personality.

Chef Hughes and chef de cuisine Josh Lauridsen, previously of Le Club Chasse et Pêche and Le Filet, prepare eclectic and adventurous variations on international classics, with an emphasis on local Quebec products. We love the energy coming from the bustling, bright kitchen in the back. From where we sit in the front of the house, we can see the team is in constant motion, and we can always spot Chef Lauridsen sporting the unique kicks that he is also known for. Bacon is a Montreal staple ingredient, and we love the chefs' summer dish of arugula, figs and ricotta sorbet atop that beloved bacon. When temperatures turn colder, we're also huge fans of the market-fresh ingredients in fall's Icelandic cod with borlotti beans and collards.

Borlotti beans
8 cups chicken stock
2 cups fresh borlotti beans
   (or dried ones, soaked
   overnight in plenty of water)
pinch of saffron

Collards
1 Tbsp canola oil
¼ cup finely chopped speck
   (or prosciutto)
2 green collard leaves,
   thinly sliced
salt and pepper

Tomato sauce
2 large tomatoes, finely chopped
2 garlic cloves, minced
¾ cup olive oil
2 Tbsp crushed croutons
1 green onion, chopped
1 Tbsp chopped fresh parsley

Radish salad
3 radishes, thinly sliced
drizzle of olive oil
drizzle of white balsamic vinegar
salt and pepper

Seared cod
4 skinless, boneless Icelandic
   cod fillets, each 5 to 6 oz
salt and pepper
¼ cup canola oil

Icelandic Cod, Borlotti Beans, Collards and Tomato Sauce

Serves four

Borlotti beans are known as cranberry beans or romano beans. If you can find them fresh (in the summer months), use them. If not, use dry beans. Speck is a northern Italian–style cured meat. If you have a hard time finding it, prosciutto is a great alternative.

Borlotti beans Bring the chicken stock to a boil in a medium pot over high heat. Add the borlotti beans and saffron and cook until the beans are soft, about 30 minutes for fresh beans or 60 to 70 minutes for dried ones. If the liquid reduces too much, add more water. Remove from the heat. Set aside the beans in the cooking juice and keep warm.

Collards Heat the canola oil in a medium frying pan over medium heat. Add the speck (or prosciutto) and cook until it renders its fat, about 3 minutes. Stir in ¼ cup of beans and some cooking liquid and the collard greens. Heat through, then season with salt and pepper. Set aside and keep warm.

Tomato sauce In a bowl, stir together the tomatoes and garlic. Fold in the olive oil until well combined. Add the croutons, green onions and parsley and stir to combine.

Radish salad In a small bowl, gently toss the radishes with the olive oil, vinegar and salt and pepper.

Seared cod Season the cod with salt and pepper. Heat the canola oil in a large frying pan over high heat. Add the cod fillets, reduce the heat to medium-high and sear on one side until golden and the flesh is firm and no longer looks raw, 6 to 8 minutes. Do not turn the fish over. You will get a nice golden crust on one side.

To serve, spoon borlotti beans and collard greens onto each plate. Place the cod on top of the beans, and garnish the fish and the plate with spoonfuls of tomato sauce. Season with salt and pepper. Serve with some of the radish salad on top.

Ricotta sorbet

¼ cup white sugar
¼ cup water
1 cup whole-milk ricotta
2 Tbsp fresh lemon juice

Arugula and fig salad

1 garlic bulb, unpeeled
3 Tbsp olive oil + a bit more for drizzling the garlic
salt and black pepper
5 Tbsp butter
1¼ cups blanched almonds
4 strips of bacon, cut lengthwise in 1-inch strips
3 Tbsp sherry vinegar
5 Tbsp canola oil
4 cups arugula
4 fresh Turkish figs, cut into 8 pieces

Serves four

Arugula and Fig Salad

Start this salad a couple of hours before you plan to serve it, so the sorbet has time to set.

Ricotta sorbet Place the sugar and water in a small pot and bring to a boil over high heat. Remove from the heat and set aside to cool to room temperature.

Measure 2 Tbsp of the simple syrup and place it in a blender (discard the rest, or reserve it for another use). Add the ricotta and lemon juice and process until smooth. Strain the mixture through a fine-mesh sieve into a shallow bowl, and then pour into an ice cream maker and process according to the manufacturer's instructions.

Arugula and fig salad Preheat the oven to 375°F. Have ready a sheet of aluminum foil. Cut the top off the head of garlic, just to expose the top of the cloves. Place the garlic in the middle of the foil, drizzle lightly with a bit of olive oil and a pinch of salt and seal tightly in the foil. Roast for 45 to 60 minutes, or until the garlic looks browned and smells sweet. Remove and set aside to cool.

Line a plate with paper towels. Melt the butter in a large frying pan over medium heat. Add the almonds and roast, stirring often, until golden. Drain off the excess butter and pour the almonds onto the paper towel–lined plate. Season them with salt. Reduce the heat to medium-low.

Return the frying pan to the stove, add the bacon and cook until crisp (or however you like it). Set aside.

Unwrap the roasted garlic and measure out 1 tsp. (The leftover roasted garlic is delicious spread on toast.) In a glass jar or a measuring cup, whisk together the vinegar, olive and canola oils and the 1 tsp of roasted garlic until well combined.

Toss together the arugula and almonds in a large salad bowl. Add the vinaigrette, mix thoroughly and season with salt and pepper. Divide the salad among 4 plates and garnish each serving with warm bacon and figs. Finish with a scoop of ricotta sorbet on top.

Gia Ba

—— *chef* ——

ANDY SU

In Taiwan, locals greet one another with *Gia ba bo*, "Have you eaten?" to which the standard reply is *Gia ba*, "We have eaten." Andy Su runs what we believe is one of the most powerful, most popular Asian kitchens in Montreal. Located in Notre-Dame-de-Grâce, a neighbourhood to the west of Montreal's downtown, it draws local families as well as many diners—including many from the restaurant industry—who appreciate the way Chef Su balances the spices in his dishes.

In a city packed with Cantonese restaurants, Gia Ba offers a taste of Taiwan, whose flavours are a unique blend of influences from several regions, and his menu combines the spiciness of Szechwan food, the sweetness of Thai cuisine and the saltiness of much Chinese cooking. Even a lightweight can handle the heat in his dishes, because the flavours hit the palate and then disappear, leaving us with a yearning for more. At Gia Ba, we are overwhelmed by the three distinct origins of Andy's Asian cooking, and at the end of the meal we have eaten—very well indeed.

1 cup dried wood ear mushrooms
2 green onions, thinly sliced
1 Tbsp minced fresh ginger
1 Tbsp minced garlic
1 tsp white sugar
4 tsp soy sauce
4 tsp Shanxi Superior Mature Vinegar
2 Tbsp chili oil
½ tsp sesame oil
¼ whole walnuts, toasted

Wood Ear Mushroom Salad with Walnuts

Serves four

Before beginning this dish, visit an Asian grocery store to buy wood ear mushrooms and Shanxi mature vinegar.

Place the mushrooms in a large bowl. Cover well with warm water and allow to reconstitute at room temperature for 10 minutes. Drain and transfer to a medium bowl.

Add the green onions, ginger, garlic, sugar, soy sauce, vinegar, chili oil, sesame oil and walnuts and toss until well combined. Serve immediately.

facing WOOD EAR MUSHROOM
SALAD WITH WALNUTS (page 57)
also pictured here top right

14 to 16 oz skinless, boneless, firm white fish, such as sablefish or tilapia, cut into ¼- to ½-inch slices

1 tsp + ¼ tsp kosher salt

1 tsp Chinese rice wine or dry sherry

1 tsp potato starch

3 Tbsp doubanjiang (Szechwan fermented chili bean paste)

2 Tbsp gochugaru (Korean chili powder) or ¼ cup chili oil

4 cups chicken stock

1 Tbsp white sugar

1 Tbsp minced fresh ginger

1 Tbsp minced garlic

1 Tbsp soy sauce

1 tsp ground + 1 tsp whole Szechwan peppercorns

3 to 4 cups bean sprouts

2 green onions, thinly sliced

1 Tbsp ground peanuts

¼ cup canola oil

10 to 20 dried Szechwan chilies or any medium dried red chilies, cut in half

Szechwan-Style Poached "White Fish"

Serves four

Szechwan food is typically hot and this is a spicy dish, but it's really not as hot as you think. All the ingredients, including the doubanjiang (Szechwan fermented chili bean paste), gochugaru (Korean chili powder), Szechwan peppercorns and Szechwan chili peppers, can be found in a good Asian grocery store. Serve this dish with lots of steamed jasmine rice.

Place the fish in a medium bowl. Stir in ¼ tsp of the salt, rice wine (or dry sherry) and potato starch. Mix until the fish is evenly coated, then cover and refrigerate for 20 to 30 minutes.

Set a wok over high heat. Add the doubanjiang, gochugaru (or chili oil), chicken stock, the 1 tsp of salt, sugar, ginger, garlic, soy sauce and ground Szechwan peppercorns. Bring to a boil, reduce the heat to medium and simmer for 2 to 3 minutes to allow the flavours to infuse.

Place a fine-mesh strainer over a clean, heatproof bowl and strain the liquid through it. Return the liquid to the stove and allow it to simmer.

Bring a medium pot of water to a boil over high heat. Add the marinated fish and blanch until mostly cooked, about 2 minutes. Transfer the fish to the simmering stock and allow to simmer for another minute.

Arrange the bean sprouts in the bottom of a large serving bowl. Ladle the fish and the stock over them, then sprinkle with the green onions and peanuts.

Heat the canola oil in a small pan over high heat. When hot, add the whole peppercorns and dried chilies, and cook until the peppercorns become aromatic and the chilies begin to brown, 1 to 2 minutes. Immediately pour the hot oil and the spices over the fish. Serve immediately.

Grumman '78

— *chef* —

MARC-ANDRÉ LECLERC

Founded in 2010, Grumman '78 is best known for leading the movement to bring street food back to Montreal. First a roaming taco truck (the Grumman truck inspired the name), and now also a full-service restaurant in St-Henri, Grumman '78 uses the tortilla as a clever base for delicious toppings. Japanese, Italian, French or Portuguese ingredients—anything goes. Turkey dinner taco? Bánh mì taco? Or all-dressed with sea snails? Like the chef, the offerings are creative and often a bit off the beaten path.

The restaurant, also known as HQ (headquarters for the food truck), is a converted old garage that once housed the city's cavalry. Stepping into the space is like walking into old Brooklyn with tables made of wooden pallets and the spools from old industrial electric wire, strings of patio lights and, hanging from the ceiling, large fishing nets drying the kitchen's hot chili peppers! Grumman '78 is the brainchild of Hilary McGown, who used to work with us at Appetite for Books, and Gaëlle Cerf and Marc-André Leclerc, both formerly of Au Pied de Cochon, among other spots. All are great hosts, and this is a place we often suggest to friends when we are a big group looking for a relaxing meal in a warm, casual atmosphere.

facing QUESADILLA ALL DRESSED

Pico de gallo

4 large ripe tomatoes, blanched, peeled and finely diced
1 small red onion, finely diced and sautéed in a little butter
juice of 1 lime
splash of red wine vinegar
dash of Valentina or Cholula hot sauce or another hot sauce of your choice
chopped fresh cilantro
splash of olive oil
salt and pepper to taste

Devilled eggs

3 large eggs
1 Tbsp mayonnaise
splash of pickle juice or white vinegar
pinch of sugar
salt to taste
smoked paprika for garnish

Taramosalata

2 slices day-old bread
¼ cup water
¼ cup milk
¼ cup carp roe "tarama"
1 tsp lemon juice + more if needed
½ small onion, finely diced
⅓ cup olive oil
salt to taste

Serves 2 to 4

Quesadilla All Dressed

Think grilled cheese when making these delicious quesadillas. A cast-iron frying pan works best so the cheese melts evenly. Whelks are a sea snail, a gastropod found in North America. Short of finding some at your fishmonger, they are not widely available. You can use canned snails (escargots) instead.

Pico de gallo In a medium bowl, mix together all the ingredients until well combined. Set aside.

Devilled eggs Have ready a bowl of ice water. Place the eggs in a small pot with cold water to cover by 1 inch, and bring to a boil over high heat. Immediately turn off the heat, and allow the eggs to sit for 15 minutes. Put the eggs in the ice water to shock them.

Peel and cut the eggs in half. Scoop out the yolk and place in a small mixing bowl. Mix in the mayonnaise, pickle juice or vinegar, and sugar, and season lightly with salt. Mix well until fully combined. Place the mixture in a piping bag and pipe into the egg whites (or spoon it back in). Dust with smoked paprika.

Taramosalata Place the bread into a bowl, pour in the water and milk and allow to soak for 1 hour. Place in a blender along with the carp roe, lemon juice and the onions. Blend on high speed and add the olive oil slowly. Once fully incorporated, adjust the seasoning. Place in a small bowl, cover and refrigerate until needed.

Whelk garlic cream

12 garlic cloves, peeled
2 cups whipping cream
salt and pepper
12 whelks, cooked and trimmed,
    or 24 canned escargots, drained
handful of chopped fresh dill

Quesadillas

8 corn tortillas, each about 6 inches
    in diameter
2 cups mixed grated cheeses (sharp
    cheddar, mozzarella, Emmenthal
    or whatever you have on hand)
Sour cream for garnish
Guacamole for garnish
1 jalapeño pepper, seeded and cut
    into rings, for garnish
3 Tbsp fancy caviar for garnish
    (optional)
2 Tbsp chopped fresh chives or green
    onions for garnish
2 to 4 lemon wedges for garnish

Whelk garlic cream Bring the garlic and cream to a boil in a small pot over high heat. Reduce the heat to medium-low and allow to simmer until the garlic is fully cooked, about 20 minutes.

Transfer the mixture to a blender (or use an immersion blender) and purée until smooth. Season with salt and pepper to taste.

Return the purée to the pot over medium-high heat, and stir in the whelks (or escargots). Bring to a gentle simmer and cook until the shellfish is warmed through, 2 to 3 minutes. Stir in the dill, reduce the heat to low and keep warm while you prepare the quesadillas.

Quesadillas Heat a large sauté pan or a cast-iron pan over medium heat. Place a tortilla in the pan, cover it with ½ cup of the mixed cheeses and set another tortilla on top. Cook on one side until the cheese is slightly melted and the tortilla becomes crispy, 3 to 4 minutes. Using a spatula, gently turn over the tortilla and cook for another 2 to 3 minutes. Transfer to an individual serving plate. Repeat with the remaining tortillas and cheese.

To serve, drown each of the quesadillas in whelk garlic cream, and spoon on some pico de gallo. Add 1 or 2 devilled eggs per quesadilla. Place a dollop of sour cream, taramosalata and guacamole, and then garnish with jalapeño rings and caviar—the more the better. Sprinkle with chives (or green onions) and enjoy with a wedge of lemon on the side.

Chocolate ganache
2½ cups chopped white chocolate
1 cup whipping cream

Cookie dough
1 cup unsalted butter, room temperature
½ cup + 2 Tbsp white sugar
4 large egg yolks, room temperature
½ Tbsp vanilla extract
1½ cups sifted all-purpose flour
1⅔ cups cornstarch
2 tsp baking powder
1 tsp baking soda
½ tsp salt

To assemble
1 cup sweetened or unsweetened shredded coconut
icing sugar for dusting

Serves 1 fatty or a small family (about 2½ dozen cookies)

Alfajores

These Latin confections, traditionally made with dulce de leche, are an all-star staple of deliciousness. Prepare the cookie dough while the chocolate ganache is cooking, and have on hand some two- to three-inch fluted cookie cutters.

Chocolate ganache Preheat the oven to 325°F. Place the chocolate and cream in a roasting pan, cover with aluminum foil and bake, stirring every 15 minutes, until pale brown throughout, about 1½ hours.

Cookie dough Place the butter in the bowl of an stand mixer fitted with a whisk attachment. Beat on high speed until very pale, about 5 minutes. Add the sugar and mix until almost white. Add the egg yolks, one at a time, followed by the vanilla.

In a large mixing bowl, combine the flour, cornstarch, baking powder, baking soda and salt. Gradually add the dry ingredients to the butter mixture, and beat on low speed just until the dough comes together. Remove it from the mixer, shape it into a flat rectangle, wrap it in plastic wrap and refrigerate the dough for 1 hour.

Preheat the oven to 325°F and line a couple of baking sheets with parchment paper. On a clean work surface, carefully roll out the cookie dough until it is ¼ inch thick. Cut the dough using fluted cookie cutters. Transfer the cookies to the baking sheets, and bake until just coloured, about 12 minutes. Remove from the oven and allow to cool.

To assemble Scoop the ganache into a piping bag. Pour the coconut onto a wide, shallow plate.

Carefully invert half of the cooled cookies and pipe the ganache onto the flat surfaces. Place an uncovered half, flat side down, over each iced cookie to form a sandwich, pressing lightly so the ganache just slightly pokes out the sides. Carefully roll each filled cookie in coconut so that it sticks to the exposed ganache. Liberally dust each cookie with icing sugar. Will keep in an airtight container at room temperature for up to 3 days.

H4C

— *chef* —

DANY BOLDUC

H4C is a beautiful restaurant set in an elegant, grey stone building that once housed a post office and bank (the wine cellar is an old bank safe!). Found in the heart of newly vibrant St-Henri, H4C was opened by Chef Dany Bolduc and two architects who restored and redesigned the space to house a large, gorgeous kitchen and a comfortable fine-dining area.

Dany grew up in Rimouski, Quebec, and is a graduate of the Institut de tourisme et d'hôtellerie du Québec in cooking (2003) and pastry (2007). His education, which included ten years of travel to more than twenty-five countries in addition to internships and work experience in both restaurants and bakeries, was a calculated plan to gain the knowledge to open his own restaurant. In 2013, after four years of leading the kitchen at Réservoir, Dany opened H4C, where his team consistently creates powerful, contemporary French gastronomy. The plating is beautiful and makes the food a delight to eat. The design, the service and the food are quintessential Dany, and we enjoy walking into his elegant restaurant and savouring what he has to offer. The snow crab is a delicate dish with a wonderful mix of flavours, and the tofu alternative to his veal sweetbread recipe is a great choice for vegetarians.

facing SNOW CRAB, DAIKON RADISH, WILD GARLIC AND GRAPEFRUIT JELLY

5 gelatin sheets
4 cups ice water
2 cups fresh grapefruit juice
¼ cup white sugar

2 cooked snow crabs
3 Tbsp grapeseed oil
1 tsp tomato paste
1 lb unsalted butter

2 large egg yolks
1 Tbsp Dijon mustard
1 or 2 drops of Tabasco sauce
1 Tbsp champagne vinegar
salt to taste
2 to 4 cups of grapeseed oil
juice of 1 lime

Snow Crab, Daikon Radish, Wild Garlic and Grapefruit Jelly

Serves four

You will need two whole snow crabs for this dish. Buy them from your local fishmonger. Cook the crab the day before you plan to make this dish so you can make the snow crab butter for the hollandaise sauce ahead of time. *Shishito* is a small, slender Japanese pepper that turns from green to red as it ripens. Look for it in Japanese food stores or substitute any mild pepper if you can't find it. Wild garlic leaves (also known as ramps) are available at specialty markets, or use spinach purée with a touch of confit garlic instead. You'll be using only two tablespoons of the H4C mayonnaise below, but it's great to have in the fridge, especially for sandwiches.

Grapefruit jelly Have ready a shallow 8-inch square glass dish.

Place the gelatin in a small bowl, cover with the ice water and allow to bloom for about 10 minutes.

While the gelatin is blooming, combine the grapefruit juice and sugar in a medium saucepan. Drain the gelatin and add it to the grapefruit juice. Bring to a boil over high heat, then remove from the heat, pour into the dish and refrigerate for at least 6 hours. Cut into ¼ to ½-inch cubes.

Snow crab butter Rinse the crabs under running water. Using a nut cracker, crack the shells and pick out the meat with a fork. Transfer the meat to a bowl, cover with plastic wrap and refrigerate until you make the salad. Using a chef's knife, chop the crab carcasses into 1-inch pieces.

Heat the grapeseed oil in a large pot over high heat until it reaches the smoking point. Add the crab carcasses and roast for about 3 minutes. Stir in the tomato paste and the butter, reduce the heat to medium-low and cook for 30 minutes without browning. Turn off the heat, cover and allow to infuse for 30 more minutes.

Snow crab salad
10 oz reserved snow crab meat
salt to taste
2 Tbsp H4C mayonnaise (recipe here)
1 fresh shishito, finely chopped
2 green onions, finely chopped
olive oil

Wild garlic purée
7 oz spinach leaves
10 wild garlic leaves (ramps)
salt
olive oil

Daikon garnish
12 thin slices daikon
salt
olive oil

Snow crab hollandaise
6 large egg yolks
¼ cup water
1 lb snow crab butter (recipe here), melted
juice of ½ lemon
2 dashes Tabasco sauce
salt to taste

Set a fine-mesh sieve over a clean bowl, pour the mixture through it and discard the solids. Set aside the sauce.

H4C mayonnaise Place the egg yolks, mustard, Tabasco sauce and champagne vinegar in a small bowl. Whisk gently until well mixed. Season with salt. Pour in the grapeseed oil, whisking continuously, until you have a mayonnaise with a semi-firm consistency. Whisk in the lime juice and set aside. (Will keep in the refrigerator for about 7 days.)

Snow crab salad Place the crabmeat in a large bowl and season with salt. Stir in the mayonnaise, the shishito, the green onions and a dash of olive oil and mix well.

Wild garlic purée Fill a large bowl with ice water.

Bring a large pot of salted water to boil over high heat. Add the spinach and wild garlic leaves and blanch for 30 seconds. Using tongs, transfer the spinach to the ice water to stop the cooking. Drain well.

Transfer the spinach and wild garlic to a blender, season with salt and olive oil and process until smooth.

Daikon garnish Place the daikon in a small bowl and season with salt and olive oil.

Snow crab hollandaise Place a large heat-proof bowl over a pot of simmering water. Using a whisk, beat the egg yolks and the water until the mixture is thick and has doubled in volume, about 3 minutes. Remove the bowl from the heat, then slowly whisk in the melted crab butter, a bit at a time, until well incorporated. Stir in the lemon juice, Tabasco and salt.

To serve, divide the wild garlic purée among 4 plates. Mound 3 "hills" of crab on each plate and cover them with a slice of daikon. Garnish with 5 cubes of grapefruit jelly and 3 spoonfuls of hollandaise. Enjoy!

*Serves
four*

Veal sweetbreads

1½ lbs veal sweetbreads, soaked
  in cold water for 24 hours
  (change the water every 8 hours)
salt
2 tsp grapeseed oil
2 Tbsp unsalted butter
1 garlic clove, crushed
1 sprig fresh thyme

Black bread crumble

4 slices black (or pumpernickel)
  bread, thinly sliced
olive oil
pinches of white sugar
salt
caraway seeds, toasted and ground
1 garlic clove, thinly sliced

Pearl onion pickle

1 bag (8 to 9 oz) pearl onions,
  peeled
1¾ cups coarse pickling salt
¼ cup white sugar
½ cup white wine vinegar
1 cup water
salt

Veal Sweetbreads with Chanterelle Mushrooms, Cauliflower and Black Bread

Use tofu as an alternative to the sweetbreads to make a quicker, vegetarian version of this dish, but be sure to choose a fresh, high-quality tofu—like the kind they sell at the Japanese grocery shop Miyamoto, in Montreal—for best results. And look for rye, caraway and coriander (black) bread at Ella's Deli, or use a good loaf of pumpernickel if you can't find it. Lemon oil is available from fine grocery stores or specialty food stores.

Veal sweetbreads Fill a large bowl with ice water. Fill a large pot with cold water, add the sweetbreads and bring to a boil over high heat. Once the water comes to a boil, drain and place the sweetbreads in the ice water to cool.

Set the sweetbreads in a meat press (set at about 2 lbs of pressure) for about 6 hours. Alternatively, place the sweetbreads on a parchment-lined baking sheet, cover with another layer of parchment and a second baking sheet and weight with heavy cans. Refrigerate for 6 hours.

Black bread crumble Preheat the oven to 275°F. Line a baking sheet with parchment paper.

Arrange the bread slices in a single layer on the baking sheet. Drizzle with olive oil and sprinkle with pinches of sugar, salt and ground caraway. Add a few garlic slices. Bake for about 30 minutes, or until the bread is thoroughly dry. Crumble gently by hand, then pulse in a spice grinder or a coffee mill. Set aside.

Pearl onion pickle Place the pearl onions in a large bowl. Add the coarse salt, mix well and set aside for 30 minutes.

Rinse the onions under running water to remove the salt. Pat dry with paper

Chanterelle mushrooms

2 tsp grapeseed oil
14 oz fresh chanterelle mushrooms
¾ cup white wine
½ cup water
1 sprig fresh thyme
1 shallot, finely chopped
1 garlic clove, minced
salt
¾ cup soy milk
dash of olive oil

Fried cauliflower

vegetable oil for deep-frying
½ head cauliflower, cut into
    marble-sized florets
salt to taste
1 tsp lemon oil

Tofu variation

10 oz high-quality semi-firm tofu
salt
cornstarch for dusting
2 tsp grapeseed oil

towels and cut into ¼-inch slices. Place the onions in a heatproof bowl and set aside.

In a large pot, bring the sugar, vinegar and water to a boil over high heat. Remove from the heat and pour the hot liquid over the onions to cover them. Allow to cool to room temperature. Drain well and set aside.

Chanterelle mushrooms Heat a frying pan over high heat. Add the grapeseed oil and swirl to coat the pan. Add the mushrooms and fry for 1 minute. Deglaze the pan with the white wine and cook until reduced completely, about 2 minutes. Stir in the water and thyme and cook until the liquid has completely evaporated, about 2 minutes. Reduce the heat to low. Add the shallots, garlic and a dash of salt and cook for about 90 seconds. Remove from the heat.

Transfer half of the mushrooms to a blender. Add the soy milk and olive oil and purée until very smooth (add a drop of water, if necessary). Set a fine-mesh sieve over a clean bowl. Strain the mushroom purée, discarding any solids, and set aside.

Fried cauliflower Line a plate with paper towels. Preheat a deep fryer to 350°F, or heat vegetable oil in a deep-sided pot until it reaches 350°F (use a deep-fry thermometer to test the temperature). Add the cauliflower and cook until golden, about 30 seconds. Using a slotted spoon, transfer the cooked cauliflower to the paper towel–lined plate to drain. Sprinkle with salt and a dash of lemon oil. Set aside.

Tofu variation Cut the tofu into 4 portions, each 2½ oz. Season well with salt.

Place the cornstarch on a large, shallow plate. Roll the tofu in cornstarch, shaking off any excess.

recipe continued overleaf...

Line a plate with paper towels. Heat the grapeseed oil in a frying pan over high heat until it reaches the smoking point. Add the tofu, reduce the heat to medium-high and cook on all sides until golden, about 2 minutes total. Transfer the tofu to the paper towel–lined plate to drain.

Finish sweetbreads Season the sweetbreads with salt. Heat the grapeseed oil in a frying pan on high heat, add the sweetbreads and sear on one side for about 45 seconds. Reduce the heat to low, add the butter, garlic and thyme and cook for about 10 minutes. Turn the sweetbreads over and cook for about 1 minute more, basting them with the melted butter.

To serve Heat the mushroom purée in a small pot over medium heat. Place the whole mushrooms and the cauliflower florets in individual pots and heat over high heat.

Divide the purée evenly among individual plates. Top with sweetbreads or tofu, then garnish with fried cauliflower, whole mushrooms and pickled onions and sprinkle with black bread crumble.

Hof Kelsten

—— *chef* ——

JEFFREY FINKELSTEIN

Jeffrey Finkelstein is our local baking hero. Raised in Côte Saint-Luc, he attended the French Culinary Institute (now the International Culinary Center) in New York City and worked as sous chef at two-star Michelin Hibiscus Restaurant in the UK and stints in several other top Michelin-starred restaurants, including El Bulli, Noma and the French Laundry. However, he's brought his talents back to Montreal at Hof Kelsten in the Plateau, which supplies high-quality bread to such acclaimed restaurants as Toqué!, Leméac and Le Club Chasse et Pêche, and provides his Jewish pastries and Eastern European deli items to regulars like us.

Much like Jeffrey himself, the bakery is modest and humble but serious about good food. The ingredients are sourced from local markets, the bread is baked in the Rolls-Royce of bread ovens right on the premises, and the atmosphere is rustic yet comfortable. It amazes us that in one place we can get high-end *pain au levain* while sipping on a warm bowl of matzo ball soup. His carefully constructed chopped liver sandwich is a favourite of ours, after which we always leave space for an authentic rugelach or a chocolate babka. As these recipes show, Jeffrey's attention to detail and passion for baking can be tasted in the end product. Who doesn't like the smell of freshly baked bread wafting through the house?

left EATING NANA'S LATKES / *facing* BIALYS

Onion topping

2 Tbsp vegetable oil
4 medium onions, finely sliced
pinch of salt
¼ cup poppy seeds

Yeasted dough

2 Tbsp olive oil + a little for
  greasing the bowl
3 cups water, room temperature
6 tsp honey
2½ tsp instant yeast
10 cups all-purpose flour
4 tsp coarse salt, like kosher,
  or fleur de sel

Makes 24 bialys

Bialys

These old-school bagel-like rolls are nice as a savoury treat in the morning, and they make an amazing brunch option when entertaining. (You can prepare the onion topping up to three days ahead and refrigerate until needed.) They originated in Białystok, Poland, but found their twentieth-century Jewish roots on the Lower East Side in New York City and are now available at our bakery's storefront in Montreal. Serve bialys at room temperature, either on their own or with cream cheese, smoked fish and/or eggs.

Onion topping Heat the vegetable oil in a frying pan over medium heat. Add the onions and salt and cook, stirring every minute, for 6 to 10 minutes or until soft and golden. Set aside to cool. Stir in the poppy seeds and refrigerate. Will keep refrigerated in an airtight container for up to 3 days.

Yeasted dough Lightly grease a large bowl with olive oil. Have ready a piece of plastic wrap large enough to cover the top of the bowl.

Warm ¾ cup + 2 tsp of the water in a small pot over medium heat until it is warm to the touch, not hot. Stir in the honey and yeast and mix well. Pour the yeast mixture into the bowl of a stand mixer fitted with a dough hook, and add the rest of the water and all of the flour on top. Mix at low speed for 2 minutes until incorporated, then increase the speed to high and mix for 4 minutes until the dough has come together and pulls away from the side of the bowl. Shape the dough into a ball, place it in the bowl, cover with plastic wrap and allow to rest for 1 hour in a warm room, away from any drafts.

With your fist, punch down the dough in the bowl, cover it again and allow it to rest in a warm place for 1 more hour.

Have ready a baking sheet lined with parchment paper. Divide the dough into 24 equal pieces and, using your hands, form them into balls. Cover and allow them to rest in a warm place for 45 minutes.

Preheat the oven to 400°F. Using your fingers, make a well in the centre of each bun, about 2 inches in diameter. (This is like making a miniature pizza with a fat crust.) Scoop a tablespoonful of the onion mixture into each well. Bake the bialys for 10 to 14 minutes, or until light golden. Remove from the oven and, while hot, brush with olive oil and sprinkle with salt.

Applesauce

4 Cortland apples (or other low-acid apple)
1 Tbsp vegetable oil
5 Tbsp white sugar
5 Tbsp cider vinegar
5 Tbsp water
5 Tbsp crème fraîche or sour cream

Latkes

3 large Idaho, russet or baking potatoes, peeled and rinsed
1 large yellow onion
1 tsp potato starch
1 large egg, beaten
1 tsp kosher salt
vegetable oil for pan-frying

Serves 8 to 12 as an appetizer

Nana's Latkes

These latkes were made "famous" by my Hungarian grandmother. They were served as she welcomed you into her home. They are revitalized at Hof Kelsten with this tangy sweet-and-sour applesauce.

Applesauce Wash and core the apples, leaving the skins on. Cut each apple into 8 wedges. Heat the vegetable oil in a medium pot over medium heat, add the apples and sauté until they soften and become golden, about 4 minutes. Set aside.

Place the sugar, vinegar and water in a small pot and bring to a boil over medium-high heat. Continue cooking until reduced by half, about 2 minutes.

Place the cooked apples and sugar-vinegar mixture in a blender and process at high speed until smooth. (You should have 1 to 1¼ cups of sauce.) Add the crème fraîche (or sour cream) and purée until smooth. Transfer to an airtight container and refrigerate for up to 2 days.

Latkes Using a box grater, coarsely grate the potatoes and onions. Transfer one-third of the grated vegetables to a food processor, add the potato starch and egg and pulse until well combined.

Place the remaining grated vegetables in a large bowl. Pour in the egg mixture, sprinkle with the salt and stir until well combined.

Line a baking sheet with paper towels. Add enough vegetable oil to a deep frying pan to cover the bottom. Heat the pan over medium heat until a pinch of latke batter dropped into the pan begins to sizzle. (If the oil does not sizzle, it is not yet hot enough; if it is smoking, turn down the heat.)

Drop heaping tablespoonfuls of the batter into the pan, working in a clockwise direction and leaving 1 inch around each latke. Turn the latkes over and cook until golden and crisp, 3 to 4 minutes per side. Transfer the cooked latkes to the paper towel–lined baking sheet to drain. Sprinkle with salt to taste. Repeat with the remaining batter.

To serve, place hot latkes on individual plates and serve with a generous dollop of applesauce.

Hôtel Herman

—— *chef* ——

MARC-ALEXANDRE MERCIER

Whenever we're considering where to go on a night out, Hôtel Herman is consistently on the list. Chef Marc-Alexandre Mercier is humble about his experience, but he's worked with some of the best, including René Redzepi at Noma, Robert Belcham at Fuel in Vancouver and Philippe Sarrail and Samuel Pinard in Montreal. The food at Hôtel Herman always features perfectly balanced flavours in which each ingredient sings to us and none overpowers the other. We order several dishes to share, and they invariably work together—the flavours light and delicate, the portions filling without leaving us feeling overstuffed.

Dominic Goyet and Ariane Lacombe, the co-owners of Hôtel Herman (along with Chef Marc-Alexandre), lead the front of the house, and their unique cocktail menu and wine list complement the food. They also carefully designed the restaurant in Mile End as a chic yet modest raw industrial space where the service is reliably top-notch without being too formal, which makes it perfect for our date nights. The menu changes with the seasons, but a couple of our favourite dishes pair rich, buttery bone marrow with salty caviar and the earthy flavour of local morels and celeriac with the clean, delicate profile of rabbit boudin blanc.

Potato purée
kosher salt
2 medium Yukon Gold potatoes
1 cup whipping cream
½ cup unsalted butter
⅓ cup whole milk

Bone marrow and new potatoes
20 new potatoes
2 Tbsp canola oil
4 marrow bones, 3 inches long and
    soaked in water for 24 hours
    (change the water twice)
juice of 1 lemon
2 Tbsp chopped fresh chives
2 Tbsp mullet caviar (or any other
    caviar)
several sprigs fresh chervil
fleur de sel

Bone Marrow with Potato Purée and Mullet Caviar

Serves four

Look for beef marrow bones at a good-quality butcher shop, and seek out mullet caviar from fine fish stores.

Potato purée Preheat the oven to 375°F. Arrange a small bed of salt on a baking sheet and place the potatoes on top. Bake for 45 to 60 minutes, or until a knife inserted into the potatoes comes out easily. Remove from the oven, and set aside until cool enough to handle. Using a paring knife, peel the potatoes. Discard the peels. Transfer the flesh to a food mill or a large bowl and mash well.

In a medium pot over medium-high heat, heat the cream, butter and milk. Stir in the mashed potato and continue stirring until the mixture is smooth and completely combined. The mixture should be creamy with the consistency of cake batter. If the purée is too wet, reduce the heat to medium and continue cooking, stirring constantly, until it thickens. Season with a generous amount of salt to taste. Reduce the heat to low and to keep warm the purée warm while you cook the bone marrow.

Bone marrow and new potatoes Preheat the oven to 400°F. Line 2 baking sheets with parchment paper.

Bring a large pot of salted water to a simmer over high heat. Add the potatoes, bring back to a simmer, reduce the heat to medium and cook for 10 minutes or until tender. Drain well. Add the canola oil, toss to combine and arrange the potatoes in a single layer on one of the baking sheets.

Remove the bones from the water and pat them dry with paper towels. Arrange the bones on the second baking sheet. Place both the potatoes and the bones in the oven, and roast for 15 to 20 minutes, or until the marrow is warmed through and soft. Remove both the bone marrow and potatoes from the oven.

In a small bowl, toss the roasted new potatoes with the lemon juice and chives.

Divide the potato purée among 4 plates. Place one bone on top of the purée and scatter the new potatoes around it. Arrange a couple of small spoonfuls of the mullet caviar over the roasted potatoes. Garnish with a few sprigs of chervil and a touch of fleur de sel over the marrow.

1 piece pre-tubed, natural hog
  casing, 6½ feet long and
  1¼ inches in diameter
15 g olive oil
125 g chopped onions
50 g day-old bread, crusts off
50 g whole milk

350 g ground rabbit thighs,
  well chilled
100 g rabbit (or pork) fat, well chilled
150 g whipping cream, well chilled
1½ large eggs, well chilled
7 g kosher salt
1 g black pepper
1 g chopped fresh thyme

½ small bay leaf
¼ cup unsalted butter
200 g fresh morels (or 60 g dried
  morels, soaked in water for
  30 minutes and then drained)
2 tsp chopped shallots
¾ cup veal stock
2 Tbsp chopped fresh chervil for
  garnish

Rabbit Boudin Blanc with Morels and Roasted Celeriac

Serves four

Boudin blanc is an emulsified sausage, and making your own is well worth the effort. Ideally, you will need a sausage stuffer to make this recipe, but if you don't have one, bake the sausage in a three- to four-cup ceramic terrine dish with a lid, placed in a roasting pan half-filled with water at 325°F for forty minutes. Visit a good-quality butcher shop to buy hog casing, rabbit thighs, rabbit (or pork) fat and veal stock. And look for celeriac, also called celery root, at farmers' markets or well-stocked produce stores.

Rabbit boudin blanc Fill a large, deep bowl with cold water. Add the hog casing and allow it to soak until it is rehydrated and well rinsed, about 1 hour.

Preheat a medium sauté pan over medium heat. Add the olive oil and onions and sauté, stirring occasionally, until the onions become translucent but not coloured. Set aside to cool.

Tear the bread into ½-inch pieces and place them in a small bowl. Pour in the milk, ensuring that it covers the bread, and allow to soak for 5 minutes.

Transfer the onions and soaked bread to the bowl of a food processor. Add the rabbit meat, rabbit (or pork) fat, cream, eggs, salt, pepper, thyme and bay leaf and process, scraping down the sides occasionally, until the mixture becomes very smooth. (You may need to do this in 2 to 3 batches.)

Place a fine-mesh sieve over a large, clean bowl. Spoon the sausage mixture into the sieve and, using the back of a large spoon, force the purée through the sieve.

Have ready 7 to 8 pieces of butcher's twine. Transfer the filling into a sausage stuffer. Rinse the hog casing in fresh water, and then thread one end of the casing onto the feeding tube of the stuffer, tie a knot at the end and pipe the meat evenly into

Roasted celeriac
1 medium celeriac, peeled
coarse salt
2 tsp sherry vinegar
4 tsp canola oil

Celeriac purée
½ medium celeriac, peeled
    and diced
2 Tbsp canola oil
kosher salt and ground black
    pepper to taste

the casing, making one long sausage about 28 inches. Once filled, tie the end off with twine.

Carefully remove the filled sausage from the stuffer, lay it on a clean work surface. Measure 4 to 5 inches from one end, pinch the filling between your thumb and forefinger, twist the casing one full rotation and tie the link with a length of butcher's twine. Repeat the twisting and tying until you reach the end of the sausage—you'll end up with about 6 sausages. Place the sausages on a plate and refrigerate to chill for 30 minutes before boiling them.

Bring a large pot of water to 160°F over medium-low heat. (Use a quick-read thermometer to test the temperature of the water, and do your best to maintain this temperature, as a higher temperature may cause the sausages to split open.) Poach the sausages for 40 minutes.

Fill a large bowl with ice water. Using a slotted spoon, gently transfer the cooked sausages to the ice water to stop the cooking. Allow them to cool in the ice water until cold, 10 to 15 minutes.

Roasted celeriac Preheat the oven to 350°F. Have ready a large sheet of aluminum foil. Wash the peeled celeriac thoroughly under cold water. Using your hands, gently rub the salt over the whole celeriac.

Place the celeriac in the middle of the sheet of aluminum foil, fold one side over the celeriac, tuck in the ends and roll the foil to completely encase the vegetable. Bake for 45 to 60 minutes, or until a wooden skewer inserted in the flesh comes out easily. Remove from the oven, remove the foil, slice into very thin rounds and set aside.

recipe continued overleaf...

Celeriac purée Preheat a medium pot over medium-high heat. When hot, sauté the celeriac in the oil for 5 minutes. Add water to cover the celeriac and bring to a simmer. Reduce the heat to medium-low, cover and allow to cook gently for 15 to 20 minutes, or until the celeriac is soft.

Strain the celeriac using a fine-mesh sieve, reserving the liquid. Place the celeriac in a blender with enough cooking water to make a smooth purée, and process, adding more cooking liquid as necessary. Season with salt and pepper. Set aside and keep warm in a small pot over low heat.

Finish boudin blanc Preheat the oven to 375°F. When ready to serve, cut 4 links from your sausage. Carefully cut through the casing and discard it. Cut each sausage into about five ½-inch pieces and place them in a bowl.

Preheat a large ovenproof sauté pan over high heat. Add 2 Tbsp of the butter and the sausages and toss gently for

30 seconds. Transfer to the oven and cook until the sausages are golden and hot all the way through, 6 to 8 minutes.

Heat a medium sauté pan over high heat. Add the remaining butter and the morels and cook, stirring often, until the morels are slightly soft and heated through, 1 to 2 minutes. Season with salt and pepper. Stir in the shallots and then pour in the veal stock. Allow the mixture to come to a boil and cook until reduced by one-quarter, about 2 minutes. Remove from the heat.

To serve Whisk together the sherry vinegar and canola oil in a small bowl. Add the celeriac and toss until well combined. Place dollops of celeriac purée and some thin slices of the roasted celeriac on each of 4 plates.

Arrange a few pieces of sausage on each plate and spoon some of the morel sauce overtop. Garnish with chervil and serve.

Icehouse

—— *chef* ——

NICK HODGE

An icehouse, at least in Texas, is a casual, open-aired shack that serves cold beer, drinks and grilled and barbecued fare. It takes its name from the days before refrigeration when ice was shipped south from Canada and the northern states and stored in hay-and-sawdust-insulated shacks, which, over time, began to sell food and ice-cold beers and sodas. The concept is still popular today, though it took Nick Hodge to bring the first icehouse to Montreal in 2010. Born into a family of caterers in Houston, Texas, Hodge opened a tiny restaurant in trendy Plateau-Mont-Royal made of ninety-year-old barn wood with two garage doors that, when opened wide in the summer, can make us feel like we're in a hut on a beach vacation even on a work night.

We love the energy at this hyper-casual forty-seater, which serves over 300 happily bourbon-soaked customers a night. The ingredients for the tacos, burritos, fried chicken, spareribs, popcorn shrimp, brisket sandwiches and po' boys—as well as many other guilty pleasures—are sourced from small local producers. Pour yourself a bourbon-spiked lemonade while you make the pimento cheese or cook up the octopus mole taco.

1 large red bell pepper
3 cups grated mild cheddar
1½ cups mayonnaise
1 shallot, finely chopped
salt and black pepper to taste
raw seasonal vegetables, such
   as carrots, celery and radishes,
   cut into bite-sized pieces

Pimento Cheese
with Crudités

*Serves
eight*

In Texas, pimento cheese is like peanut butter. Though it's generally not served with jelly, it is found in most Texan kids' lunch boxes. In my house it was the go-to after-school snack, too, served on crackers, on celery, on white bread with butter, or—don't judge—straight out of the jar. Here, it's gussied up with raw seasonal vegetables.

Preheat the broiler to high. Place the bell pepper on a baking sheet and place it directly under the broiler. Allow to char, turning occasionally, until the flesh is dark all the way around, 5 to 7 minutes. Remove from the oven, place in a bowl, cover with plastic wrap and allow to cool for 30 minutes.

Using your hands, remove and discard the charred skin and seeds. Finely dice the bell pepper and place it in a medium bowl. Add the cheese, mayonnaise and shallots and mix until well combined. Season with salt and a good amount of ground black pepper. Scoop the pimento cheese into a small ramekin and serve on a platter with the crudités.

1 frozen octopus, 5 to 7 lbs, thawed

1 large carrot

¼ cup + 2 Tbsp olive oil

1 garlic bulb, cloves separated and peeled

4 dried ancho chilies

3 sprigs fresh Mexican oregano (or ¼ cup dried)

20 to 28 corn tortillas, each 6 inches in diameter

1 cup crumbled queso fresco or crumbled feta for garnish

chopped cilantro for garnish

ingredients continued…

Octopus Mole Tacos with Fried Brussels Sprouts

Serves 10 to 14

Mole is a complex Mexican sauce made with dried chilies, nuts and dried fruits and heavily flavoured with a variety of spices. There are about as many recipes for mole as there are people who make it. This recipe is for *mole negro*, or "black mole." Its deep colour and rich flavour come from burning the chili seeds. Don't be afraid to really darken the mole fixings. That being said, the process of blackening the chili seeds creates *a lot* of smoke (think pepper spray). Open your windows and doors! Look for the dried chilies, Mexican oregano, queso fresco and Mexican chocolate in any good Latin American grocery store or specialty food shop.

Fried is my favourite way to eat Brussels sprouts; however, it is also the most dodgy way to prepare them. As soon as you drop the leaves into the hot oil, they go freakin' nuts popping for a few seconds. Before you start, make yourself a "pop zone," free of clutter, where you can take refuge. Drop the sprouts into the oil, and JUMP BACK!

Braised octopus tacos Rinse the octopus thoroughly under cold water, removing and discarding, if present, the ink sacs, beak, gills and entrails. Using a sharp knife, cut the cape from the base of the 8 tentacles. Discard the cape. Cut the tentacles from one another.

Place the tentacles on a clean work surface. Working with one tentacle at a time, beat the tentacle from end to end with the carrot to tenderize it. Beat each tentacle semi-aggressively for about 5 minutes. (You don't want to beat the octopus too hard or it will become mushy when cooked. If the carrot breaks, you're hitting too hard.) Discard the carrot.

Preheat the oven to 350°F. Heat a large ovenproof pot over high heat, then add ¼ cup of the olive oil. Working in batches, sear the tentacles until they begin to curl, 45 to 60 seconds each. Transfer the seared tentacles to a clean plate and repeat until all the octopus has been cooked. (Do not

recipe continued overleaf…

Mole sauce

2 dried ancho chilies
2 dried mulato chilies
2 dried guajillo chilies
1 lb tomatillos, husks removed (about 6)
1 large tomato
1 medium Spanish onion, peeled and quartered
4 garlic cloves, peeled
4 corn tortillas, each 6 inches in diameter
4 sprigs fresh cilantro

½ cup dried cherries
¼ cup dried apricots
2 dried figs
3 oz Mexican chocolate tablet, roughly chopped
1 tsp ground cinnamon
1 tsp ground allspice
1 Tbsp ground cumin
1 Tbsp toasted sesame seeds
¼ cup pecan halves
4 cups dark chicken stock
salt and pepper to taste

overcrowd the pot.) Add the garlic, chilies and Mexican oregano to the pot. Stir in the octopus, cover and cook in the oven for 1 to 1½ hours. The octopus is done when a wooden skewer inserted into the largest piece meets no resistance. Remove from the oven, uncover the pot and allow it to cool slightly. Refrigerate the octopus in its own juices for 12 to 24 hours.

Remove the tentacles from the pot and cut them into ¼-inch slices on the diagonal. Discard the cooking juices. (Alternatively, leave them whole, brush them with olive oil and sear them on a charcoal grill rather than pan-frying them on the stove.)

Heat the remaining 2 Tbsp olive oil in a large frying pan over high heat. Add the tentacles and sear for 1 to 2 minutes, or until they are lightly caramelized. (You just want to give them a little colour and crispness.)

Mole sauce Preheat the oven to 425°F. Arrange the dried chilies on a baking sheet in a single layer (do not stack them). Roast for 5 minutes. Remove from the oven, allow to cool and then remove and discard the chili stems. Using your hands, separate the seeds from the pods and reserve both in separate bowls.

Open all of the windows in your home. Seriously. Open all the doors, too. Heat a dry cast-iron frying pan over high heat until ripping hot. Add the chili seeds and roast them, shaking the pan occasionally, until they start to smoke and turn black, 3 to 4 minutes. Pour the blackened seeds into a small bowl.

Return the frying pan to the heat, add the tomatillos, tomato, onions and garlic and cook, turning occasionally, until the vegetables begin to blister and blacken, about 5 minutes. Transfer the vegetables to a bowl.

Return the frying pan to the heat, add the tortillas and toast them on both sides until slightly burnt, about 1 minute per side.

Combine all of the mole ingredients in a large, heavy-bottomed stockpot and cook over medium heat until the vegetables are softened, 20 to 25 minutes. Using an immersion blender or a stand blender, blend the mole until smooth. For

Pickled red onions

1 cup plain white vinegar
1 cup cold water
2 Tbsp white sugar
2 Tbsp kosher salt
1 large red onion, julienned
½ tsp toasted cumin seeds

Fried Brussels sprouts

3 cups canola oil for frying
1 lb Brussels sprouts, outer leaves
    peeled and cores quartered
¼ cup thinly sliced green onions
¼ cup fresh cilantro leaves
salt and black pepper to taste

an even smoother texture, strain the mole through a fine-mesh sieve and discard the solids. Will keep refrigerated in an airtight container for 5 days.

Pickled red onions Place the vinegar, water, sugar and salt in a medium non-reactive (e.g., stainless steel) saucepan and bring to a boil over high heat. Add the onions and cumin seeds and allow to boil for 2 minutes. Remove from the heat and cool to room temperature. Will keep refrigerated in an airtight container for up to 1 month.

Fried Brussels sprouts Line a large plate with paper towels. Heat the canola oil in a large cast-iron pot over medium-high heat until it reaches 350°F. (Use a deep-fry thermometer to check the temperature.) Clear an area about 6 feet wide in all directions from the pot: this will be the "pop zone."

Using a slotted spoon, carefully drop a handful of Brussels sprouts into the hot oil and quickly take refuge in the "pop zone." The Brussels sprouts will pop wildly for 2 to 3 seconds. Allow the Brussels sprouts

to cook for 2 minutes, or until they are golden and crispy. Transfer them to the paper towel–lined plate. Repeat with the remaining Brussels sprouts, working in batches, until they are all cooked.

Transfer the Brussels sprouts to a large bowl, add the green onions and cilantro and toss well. Season to taste with salt and black pepper.

Finish tacos Heat a dry cast-iron frying pan over medium-high heat. Place 2 tortillas, one on top of the other, in the pan and cook on one side for 1 minute to slightly crisp the outside. Turn the tortillas over, keeping one on top of the other, and cook for another minute. (Each tortilla will be toasty on one side, steamy and soft on the other.)

Place each tortilla, soft side up, on a plate and spread it with a spoonful of the mole sauce. Top the tortilla with a few slices of the octopus and Brussels sprouts, and then garnish with pickled red onions, cheese and cilantro. Repeat with the remaining tacos and toppings. Serve 2 tacos per person.

Impasto

— chef —

STEFANO FAITA
AND MICHELE FORGIONE

Stefano Faita and Michele Forgione are the team behind Impasto, our go-to restaurant for authentic Italian cuisine. As a young boy, Stefano peeped out from behind the counter of his family's business, Quincaillerie Dante, and he's gone on to author three cookbooks, host three television shows, run the Mezza Luna cooking school with his mom and open two restaurants with Michele just across the street from his family's shop. Michele has led the kitchen at several Montreal restaurants, and his talented touch is evident at Impasto and Pizzeria Gema.

We love heading to Little Italy, where the sound of Italian being spoken in the streets and Michele's fresh homemade pasta instantly transport us to *il bel paese*. His signature Sunday sauce is a family recipe from his mother, Filomena, and though it takes some time to prepare, it is perfect for a rainy or snowy Sunday when you want to treat your family and friends to an Italian feast. Stefano's porchetta recipe, which is a staple on the Impasto menu, can be your *secondi* that evening. *Buon appetito!*

facing PORCHETTA

2 Tbsp chopped fresh thyme
2 Tbsp chopped fresh rosemary
2 Tbsp chopped fresh sage
1 Tbsp fennel seeds, crushed
1 tsp dried chili flakes
5 garlic cloves, chopped
2 Tbsp white wine
6 Tbsp olive oil + more for the outside
   of the pork
salt and freshly ground pepper
5 to 6 lbs boneless pork shoulder

Serves 8 to 10

Porchetta

Porchetta is a celebratory spice-stuffed pork roast often served with rapini as a main course or sliced and tucked into sandwiches with roasted bell peppers and salsa verde. For the best flavour—and to save time when hosting—prepare this dish the day before you plan to serve it.

Preheat the oven to 425°F. Have ready about 6 pieces of butcher's twine, each about one arm's length long.

In a small bowl, combine the thyme, rosemary, sage, fennel seeds, chili flakes, garlic, white wine and 6 Tbsp of olive oil. Season with salt and pepper and mix well. Set aside.

To butterfly the pork, place it on a clean work surface. Set one hand on top of the meat. Using a very sharp knife, slice horizontally through the roast, being careful not to completely separate the 2 pieces. Gently open up the pork shoulder like a book. You may need to do this bit by bit, gradually pulling the meat open with one hand while cutting with the other. You want to have one big piece of equal thickness. Rub the herb paste evenly into the cut side of the pork.

Using your hands and starting at one edge, tightly roll up the pork. Tie 6 pieces of butcher's twine around the roast to seal in the filling, then season the pork with salt and pepper, rub the outside lightly with olive oil and transfer to a roasting pan. Roast for 15 minutes, then reduce the heat to 300°F and continue to roast until the meat is medium-well (the internal temperature reaches 155°F to 160°F on a meat thermometer), 1½ to 2 hours. (To crisp the skin, remove the roast from the oven, and then preheat the broiler. Return the roast to the oven until the skin is golden, 3 to 5 minutes.)

Remove the pork from the oven, cover it loosely with aluminum foil and allow it to rest for 15 to 20 minutes. Untie the roast and discard the kitchen twine, then slice the porchetta into rounds 1 inch thick.

Sunday sauce

2 Tbsp olive oil

1 lb pork spareribs, cut into 1- or
  2-bone pieces, patted dry

2 veal blade steaks, whole

1 lb mild Italian sausage, whole

4 garlic cloves, peeled and left whole

¼ cup tomato paste

3 cans (each 28 oz) peeled whole
  Italian tomatoes, puréed or roughly
  chopped

2 cups water

salt and pepper

6 leaves fresh basil, torn into
  small pieces

1 lb fresh cavatelli, rigatoni,
  pasta shells or a mix

freshly grated romano cheese
  for garnish

Pasta with Meatballs in Sunday Sauce

Serves 8 to 10

In the restaurant, we purée the tomatoes for the Sunday sauce using a food mill or an immersion blender. If you prefer a chunkier, more rustic version, roughly chop the tomatoes instead. Prepare the meatballs and the pasta while the sauce is simmering. It's traditional to serve the pasta with just the meatballs, but if you also want to serve the cooked spareribs, veal and sausage, by all means do so!

Sunday sauce Have ready a large plate. Heat the olive oil in a large, heavy pot over medium heat. Add the pork ribs and cook, turning the pieces occasionally, for about 15 minutes or until nicely browned on all sides. Using a slotted spoon, transfer the cooked pork to the plate.

Add the veal to the pot and cook, turning the pieces occasionally, for about 8 minutes or until nicely browned on all sides. Add the cooked veal to the plate.

Place the sausages in the pot and cook until browned on all sides, about 3 minutes. Transfer the sausages to the plate with the veal and pork. Drain off most of the fat from the pot, then add the garlic and cook for about 2 minutes or until golden. Remove and discard the garlic. Stir in the tomato paste and cook for 1 minute. Pour in the puréed (or roughly chopped) tomatoes and their juice, then add the water and season with salt and pepper to taste. Add the pork, veal and sausages and the basil and bring the sauce to a simmer. Partially cover the pot, reduce the heat to low and cook, stirring occasionally, for 2 hours. If the sauce becomes too thick, add a little more water.

Meatballs

1 lb ground beef (or a combination
   of beef and pork)
½ cup dried bread crumbs
2 large eggs
1 tsp minced garlic
½ cup freshly grated romano or
   Parmesan
2 Tbsp finely chopped fresh flat-leaf
   parsley
1 tsp kosher salt
black pepper
2 Tbsp olive oil

Meatballs In a large bowl, combine all of the ingredients except the olive oil. Using your hands, mix thoroughly until well combined. Rinse your hands with cool water, then gently scoop a few tablespoonfuls of the mixture into your palm and lightly shape it into a 2-inch ball. Repeat with the remaining meat. (You should have 8 to 10 meatballs.)

Have ready a large plate. Heat the olive oil in a large, heavy sauté pan over medium-high heat. Add the meatballs, in batches if necessary, and brown them well on all sides, about 3 minutes. Don't be concerned if they are still raw in the middle; they will finish cooking in the sauce. Transfer the meatballs to a plate.

Finish sauce Once the sauce has cooked for 2 hours, add the meatballs and cook for 30 minutes or until the sauce is thick and the meats are very tender.

Just before serving, bring a large pot of salted water to a boil over high heat. Add the pasta and cook until al dente. Remove all the meat and meatballs from the sauce and set aside. Drain the pasta once ready and add it to the sauce and stir. Divide the pasta in individual bowls, add a few meatballs, sprinkle with freshly grated romano cheese and serve hot.

Jun-i

—— chef ——

JUNICHI IKEMATSU

Chef Junichi Ikematsu was born in Kyoto, and he began his culinary career early by joining the brigade of Manyoken, a highly regarded French restaurant in that city. He later moved to Kobe before a friend convinced him to move to Montreal, where trained Japanese chefs were in short supply. He rapidly built his reputation at Soto and then opened his own restaurant, Jun-i, in Mile End in 2005. Since then, Jun-i has consistently impressed us with a masterful sushi menu but especially with its non-traditional offerings, dishes that combine sweetbreads, grilled quail, black truffle oil, foie gras, veal stock and beurre blanc sauce with Japanese technique and ingredients.

Chef Juni is a purist. He cooks on a grill imported from Japan, and the majority of his fish is flown in directly from the Fukuoka market in Kyushu. It's this attention to detail—as well as his meticulously prepared yet innovative dishes—that have made the restaurant a favourite of many in the restaurant industry. When we visit, we always pick a sweetbread dish because his take varies with the seasons, a ravioli dish because it is always surprisingly different and, of course, a variety of sashimi and maki. And when we're in the mood for a simple bowl of authentic ramen noodles, we stop by Saka-Ba!, his recently opened paean to Japanese soul food.

Tosazu sauce

3 Tbsp + 1 tsp sake
3 Tbsp + 1 tsp soy sauce
⅓ cup + 1 Tbsp rice vinegar
3 Tbsp + 1 tsp mirin
1 Tbsp white sugar
pinch of katsuobushi
    (bonito flakes) (optional)

Yuzu-miso sauce

¼ cup white miso paste
2 Tbsp sake
1 large egg yolk
¼ cup white sugar
¼ cup yuzu juice

Yuzu cream

1 shallot, finely chopped
zest of 1 orange
½ cup tosazu sauce (recipe here)
2 Tbsp maple syrup
3 Tbsp yuzu juice
½ cup whipping cream

Hamachi

1 lb sashimi-grade yellowtail
    tuna fillet, chilled and very thinly
    cut into 5 to 6 slices per person
handful of baby mesclun
segments from 1 orange

Hamachi Yuzu-Miso Yaki
(Grilled Yellowtail Tuna with Yuzu-Miso Glaze)

Serves six

Yaki means "grilled" in Japanese, and this dish is prepared using a culinary torch. *Hamachi* is the Japanese word for yellowtail tuna, which is served raw in this recipe. Visit your fishmonger and ask for the freshest, sashimi-grade fish available, keep it well chilled before serving and be sure your hands, kitchen and utensils are very clean when you handle it. Pick up white miso (fermented soybean paste), sake (rice wine), yuzu juice, rice vinegar, mirin (sweet rice wine) and katsuobushi (dried bonito flakes) from a Japanese food store. Use leftover tosazu sauce as a salad dressing.

Tosazu sauce Bring the sake, soy sauce, rice vinegar, mirin and sugar to a boil in a small saucepan over high heat. Remove from the heat, add the bonito flakes and allow to sit for 30 minutes. Strain the mixture through a fine-mesh sieve into a clean bowl. Discard the solids. Will keep refrigerated in an airtight container for up to 5 days.

Yuzu-miso sauce Place the miso, sake, egg yolk and sugar in a small saucepan over medium-low heat. Cook, stirring constantly with a spoon until the mixture reaches 90°F (use an instant-read thermometer) and becomes creamy, about 5 minutes. Remove from the heat and strain the mixture through a fine-mesh sieve into a clean bowl. Discard the solids. Stir in the yuzu juice until well combined. Will keep refrigerated in an airtight container for up to 5 days.

Yuzu cream In a small bowl, whisk all the ingredients until well combined.

Hamachi Arrange the fish in a single layer on a plate, and brush generously with the yuzu-miso sauce. Using a food torch, grill the fish for 5 to 10 seconds until the sauce is golden. (If you do not have a food torch, skip this step.)

To serve, arrange the mesclun on a serving platter. Place the fish on top, drizzle with some of the yuzu cream and garnish the platter with orange segments. Serve immediately.

Cilantro and parsley pesto
1 shallot
½ cup olive oil
½ cup fresh cilantro
½ cup fresh parsley

Nori paste
4½ sheets of nori, cut into pieces
¾ cup + 4 tsp water
¾ cup + 4 tsp sake
¼ cup soy sauce
5 Tbsp white sugar

Sea bass tartare
12 to 14 oz skinless, boneless
    European sea bass, striped bass or
    red snapper fillet, cut in small dice
1 Tbsp chopped walnuts
1 Tbsp chopped dried cranberries
salt and black pepper to taste
1 Tbsp flying fish roe for garnish
1 Tbsp smelt roe for garnish (optional)
6 Tbsp chopped fresh cilantro (or
    edible flowers or micro greens)
good-quality olive oil for garnish

Suzuki Tarutaru
(Sea Bass Tartare)

Sea bass, flying fish roe and smelt roe are available from your local specialty fishmonger. Look for nori (thin, dried sheets of seaweed) in Japanese food stores or in the international aisle of your grocery store, and sake at the SAQ or your local fully stocked liquor store. Have handy a two- to three-inch round cookie cutter or ring mould. Serve with crostini.

Cilantro and parsley pesto Mix together all of the ingredients in a blender and set aside. Will keep refrigerated in an airtight container for up to 2 days.

Nori paste In a small bowl, whisk together all of the ingredients and allow to sit for 5 to 10 minutes at room temperature. The mixture will thicken to a pasty consistency. Will keep refrigerated in an airtight container for up to 10 days.

Sea bass tartare In a bowl, combine the sea bass (or snapper), walnuts, cranberries and 2 Tbsp of the cilantro and parsley pesto. Season to taste with salt and black pepper.

Place the cookie cutter (or ring mould) in the middle of a serving plate, and fill with 2 to 3 oz of tartare. Carefully remove the cutter (or mould), then top the tartare with 1 Tbsp nori paste and sprinkle with ½ tsp of the fish roe, ½ tsp of the smelt roe (if using) and 1 Tbsp of the cilantro (or edible flowers or micro greens). Drizzle with olive oil.

Junior

— chef —
DRÉ (ANDRÉ) MEJIA

One of the most talked-about recent openings, Junior brings Filipino street food to Montreal's Griffintown. This casual forty-seater restaurant is the brainchild of brothers (and DJs) Jojo and Toddy Flores with Dr. Julian Somera and sommelier David Pendon, and it combines their passions. The soundtrack includes a nice mix of underground house and hip hop, the bar offers a unique natural wine and microbrewery beer program and the kitchen serves up classic dishes such as *lumpia*, pork adobo and fried *ukoy*. The small, bright space is always fun and always lively.

Although Chef Dré (André) Mejia trained in Italian cooking at the one-star Michelin Met Restaurant in Venice, here he draws on his Filipino heritage and his experience creating authentic *carinderia*, or open-air market, food in Toronto. We love the sweetness of the *buto-buto* dry honey spareribs and the crispy pork belly to start, and the *pancit* (rice noodles sautéed with veggies, chicken and shrimp) are nice and light with a perfect balance of flavours. If you can't get to the restaurant, turn up the house music, pull out these recipes and get cooking!

¾ cup cane vinegar

¼ cup dark soy sauce

1 Tbsp white sugar

½ Tbsp kosher salt

1 Tbsp black peppercorns, coarsely ground

1 lemon grass stalk, cut in half and bruised with the back of a knife

4 to 4½ lbs boneless pork shoulder, well marbled, cut into 1-inch cubes

½ cup canola (or vegetable) oil

1 garlic bulb, cloves separated, peeled and crushed

2 bay leaves

1 cup chicken stock

Adobong Baboy
(Pork Adobo)

Serves 6 to 8

Cane vinegar is a staple ingredient in Philippine cooking. The juice from sugar cane is extracted, simmered and then fermented to create a delicate vinegar with a balanced sour and sweet flavour. Look for it at any good Asian grocery store, or substitute unseasoned rice vinegar. Serve this classic Filipino dish with bowls of steamed white jasmine rice.

Combine the vinegar, soy sauce, sugar, salt and pepper and lemon grass in a large bowl until well mixed. Add the pork, cover and refrigerate for 12 to 24 hours.

Remove and discard the lemon grass. Remove the pork from the marinade, shaking off any excess marinade, and pat it dry with paper towels. Reserve and set aside the marinade.

Heat the canola (or vegetable) oil in a large pot over high heat. Add the pork, in batches, if necessary, and brown the meat on all sides, about 5 minutes total. Using a slotted spoon, transfer the meat to a plate. Repeat until all the meat is cooked. Pour off and discard the fat, leaving roughly 1 Tbsp.

Reduce the heat to medium and return the pot to the stove. Stir in the garlic and sauté, stirring continuously so it does not colour, for about 1 minute. Pour in the reserved marinade, increase the heat to medium-high and scrape any browned bits that are sticking to the bottom of the pan. Stir in the bay leaves and chicken stock, add the pork and increase the heat to high. When the mixture comes to a boil, reduce the heat to medium and allow the pork to simmer for 45 minutes to 1 hour, or until the meat is fork tender. Season to taste with salt and pepper. Ladle into bowls and serve.

Licence Complète - Fully Licensed
FILIPINO SPECIALITIES
JUNIOR
SPÉCIALITÉS PHILIPPINES

1 package (8 oz) pancit bihon noodles
2 chicken legs (or 1 chicken breast),
  skin on
2 Tbsp canola (or vegetable) oil
3 garlic cloves, minced
¼ head green cabbage, shredded
1 carrot, cut into thin matchsticks
¾ cup celery, cut into thin matchsticks

¾ cup snow peas
¼ cup cooked small shrimp
  salt and pepper to taste
1 Tbsp patis (fish sauce)
3 Tbsp dark soy sauce
⅓ cup chopped green onions
5 calamansi limes or 1 large lime,
  sliced

Pancit Bihon
(Filipino Fried Noodles)

Serves 4 to 6

Pancit bihon noodles, *patis* (fish sauce) and calamansi limes can be found at any good Asian grocery store. You can substitute thin rice vermicelli noodles for the pancit bihon noodles, Thai fish sauce for the patis and regular limes for the calamansi ones.

Bring a large pot of water to a boil over high heat. Add the noodles and cook for 2 minutes. Drain the noodles in a colander, run them under cold water, drain again and set aside.

Fill the same pot with water, add the chicken and return to high heat. Cook for about 30 minutes, or until the meat is tender and easily comes away from the bones. Using a slotted spoon, transfer the chicken to a plate to cool. Measure 2 cups of the cooking stock and set aside. When the chicken is cool enough to handle, pull the meat from the bones, and discard the skin and bones.

Heat the canola (or vegetable) oil in a wok or a large sauté pan over high heat. Add the garlic and sauté for about 10 seconds. Stir in the cabbage, carrots, celery and snow peas and cook for 2 minutes. Add the cooked chicken and shrimp and season with salt and pepper. Pour in the reserved chicken stock and the cooked noodles and stir gently. Add the fish sauce and soy sauce and cook until heated through, about 3 minutes.

Transfer the noodles to a large serving platter and garnish with green onions. Serve family-style with the lime on the side so your guests can squeeze the juice over their plate before eating.

Lavanderia

—— *chef* ——

ANTONIO PARK,
TAKESHI HORINOUE AND
PAUL MAURICE POSADA

(not shown)

A laundromat in Westmount might sound like an unusual place to eat, but Lavanderia is a *parrilla* inspired by Chef Antonio Park's childhood. A departure from the predominantly Japanese and Korean flavours for which he is so well known at Park (page 176), the new restaurant is just two doors down from his flagship and named for the factory Park's father owned in Argentina that produced the acid wash and stonewash finish for top American jeans brands. There, at lunchtime, the family joined hundreds of people for a staff meal of blood sausage, chorizo, ribs, sweetbreads and whole cows grilled over the gnarled roots of a mango tree.

At Lavanderia, white walls reach thirty feet high to create a large, airy room with space for laundry lines hung with seasonal artwork. The unpretentious atmosphere showcases a colourful tapas-style menu where grilled meats, or *asado*, are the specialty. We love the rich smoky flavour of grilled short ribs, which are cooked in a charcoal- and wood-burning oven and served with homemade condiments like chimichurri. And we never hesitate to order the grilled sweetbreads, which are a gorgeous balance of sweet, salty and charred flavours. As with the food at all of his restaurants, the *Chopped Canada* judge continues to blow it out of the park, and his dedicated and talented co–chefs de cuisine Takeshi Horinoue and Paul Maurice Posada are always there to take his lead.

facing MILANESA DE POLLO CON QUESO

Tomato salsa

1 small onion, finely diced
2 plum tomatoes, seeded and diced
¼ cup chopped fresh parsley
¼ cup chopped fresh cilantro
2 Tbsp chopped fresh oregano
1 garlic clove, minced
1 Tbsp sweet paprika
½ cup extra-virgin olive oil
salt and black pepper

Breaded chicken cutlets

2 large skinless, boneless chicken
  breasts
¾ cup all-purpose flour
3 large eggs, beaten
3 cups panko bread crumbs
2 cups canola oil

Milanesa de Pollo con Queso
(Breaded Chicken Cutlets with Cheese)

Serves four

In Argentina, *milanesa* is a very traditional homestyle dish that has as many variations as there are households. This is Chef Antonio's favourite version—the one that he grew up with. Queso blanco and ricotta salata are fresh dry cheeses typically found in Mexican and Italian grocery stores.

Tomato salsa Place all of the ingredients in a large bowl and stir to combine. Season to taste with more salt and black pepper. Cover and set aside.

Breaded chicken cutlets Have ready 2 large sheets of plastic wrap and a meat mallet. Arrange the chicken breasts on a clean cutting board, and using a sharp knife, cut them in half horizontally. You should end up with 2 large, flat cutlets per breast.

Place one cutlet at a time between the 2 large pieces of plastic wrap. Using the meat mallet, pound the cutlet until it is ¼ inch thick. Repeat with the remaining cutlets. Set aside.

Arrange the flour on a large plate. Place the eggs in a large shallow bowl, big enough to hold the cutlets. Set the bread crumbs on a second large plate. Working with one cutlet at a time, dredge the chicken completely in the flour, then in the egg and finally in the bread crumbs. Place the breaded chicken on a plate and repeat with the remaining cutlets.

Pour the canola oil into a large deep-sided frying pan, and preheat it to 350°F over medium-high heat. (Use a deep-fry thermometer to test the temperature.) Line a baking sheet with paper towels.

Simple crostini
4 slices sourdough bread, each
    ½ inch thick
olive oil to drizzle
unsalted butter, room temperature
salt and black pepper
1 medium plum tomato, thinly sliced
½ cup crumbled queso blanco or
    ricotta salata
micro greens for garnish

Working with one cutlet at a time, gently lower it into the hot oil and cook until golden brown, 4 to 5 minutes. Using tongs or a slotted spoon, transfer the cooked cutlet to the paper towel–lined plate to drain. Repeat with the remaining cutlets. Set aside.

Simple crostini Preheat a grill to medium or preheat the oven to 400°F.

Arrange the bread slices on an oven-proof plate, drizzle olive oil over them and apply a thin layer of butter. Season lightly with salt and pepper. Grill the bread directly over medium heat or toast in the oven for 7 minutes. Remove and set aside.

To serve Place a crostini on each plate and 2 to 3 slices of tomato on top. Sprinkle some queso blanco (or ricotta salata) over the tomato, and then cover it with a chicken cutlet. Spoon a generous portion of the tomato salsa on top and sprinkle with some of the micro greens to garnish. Serve immediately.

¼ cup olive oil

2 lbs veal osso buco, crosscut 1 inch thick

1 lb stewing beef, cut into 2-inch cubes

10 to 11 oz pork belly, cut into 2-inch cubes

salt and black pepper

3 garlic cloves, chopped

4 medium carrots, cut in large dice

2 medium white onions, chopped

3 leeks, white part only, cut into 1-inch slices

6 medium potatoes, peeled and cut in large dice

1 small pumpkin or any type of winter squash, peeled, seeded and cut in 2-inch dice

3 ears fresh corn, cut into 2-inch rounds

3 celery stalks, cut in large dice

2–3 good-quality semi-dry chorizo sausages (sweet or spicy), divided into 6 pieces

⅓ bunch fresh flat-leaf parsley, roughly chopped

Argentinean Puchero

Serves 6 to 8

Puchero is a type of stew cooked in every household in Argentina, where Chef Antonio Park grew up. The use of beef and corn makes this version distinctly Argentinean. Try this one-pot peasant dish in the winter months to warm you up. The mixture of meats and vegetables seems simple, but the flavours are complex and exciting. Serve with slices of crusty fresh bread.

Heat a large heavy-bottomed pot or Dutch oven over high heat, and add enough olive oil to coat the bottom. Season the osso buco, stewing beef and pork belly with salt and black pepper. As soon as the pot starts to smoke, add the osso buco in a single layer, without crowding the pot, and cook until well browned, about 5 minutes per side. Transfer the osso buco to a plate. Repeat the browning process with the beef and pork belly.

Pour off the excess fat from the pot, leaving 2 Tbsp. Reduce the heat to low, add the garlic and sauté for 30 seconds. Return the meat to the pot and add just enough water to cover. Increase the heat to high, allow the water to come to a boil and, using a spoon, skim off any impurities that rise to the top. Reduce the heat to medium-low and simmer for 1 hour, uncovered. Stir in the carrots and onions and simmer for another hour, or until the meats are fork tender and easily pull apart.

Add the leeks, potatoes, pumpkin, corn, celery and chorizo. Increase the heat to medium, bring to a simmer and cook for 20 minutes. As soon as all the vegetables and chorizo are cooked though, season with salt and black pepper to taste. Finish with the parsley.

Léché Desserts

—— chef ——

JOSIE WEITZENBAUER

The main floor of an old luggage factory in St-Henri may not sound like a likely spot to find some of Montreal's most delicious doughnuts, but it is. Tucked among the exposed bricks and beams of this industrial building is an open kitchen in which pastry chef Josie Weitzenbauer and her team create their signature dish in a dazzling array of flavours, from pistachio cream and sesame miso to lemon meringue, passionfruit glaze and double chocolate brownie.

Through the huge paned windows come the sounds of trains chugging by, kids playing in the park across the street, cyclists whizzing by en route to the canal. This busy yet relaxed atmosphere is a far cry from Josie's crazy days of training in high-end restaurants across Europe and Canada, creating beautiful, elaborate desserts while hidden away in the corner of a kitchen. We are big fans of Léché doughnuts in their signature hot-pink boxes. Everything is made in-house from the freshest ingredients, and we always look forward to the latest seasonal offerings.

Rosewater white chocolate mousse
2 ⅔ cups chopped white chocolate
3 gelatin sheets
2 cups water, ice cold
3 large egg yolks
1 cup milk
1 cup + 2 ⅓ cups whipping cream
1 tsp rosewater

*Serves 12
(makes 50
beignets)*

Rosewater White Chocolate Beignets with Streusel

You can also prepare the streusel and the white chocolate filling ahead of time and refrigerate them until needed. And for more effect, garnish the beignets with turkish delight, tempered chocolate curls and fresh rose petals. *Voilà!*

Rosewater white chocolate mousse Place the white chocolate in a large, heatproof stainless steel bowl. Bring a large pot of water to a simmer over medium heat and set the bowl of chocolate over it.

While the chocolate is melting, place the gelatin in a small bowl, add the water and allow to bloom. Set aside. Remove the melted chocolate from the heat and set aside.

Place the egg yolks in a medium bowl. In a medium saucepan, bring the milk and 1 cup of the cream to a boil over medium heat. Watch closely so it does not boil over! Slowly pour the mixture over the yolks, whisking constantly. Pour the custard mixture back into the saucepan, return to the heat and cook until it reaches 175°F.

Squeeze as much excess water as you can from the gelatin. Whisk the gelatin and the rosewater into the hot custard mixture, then pour it over the melted chocolate. Mix until well combined. Allow the mixture to cool to room temperature, stirring occasionally.

In the bowl of a stand mixer fitted with a whisk attachment, whip the 2 ⅓ cups of whipping cream at medium speed until they form soft peaks. Gently fold the whipped cream into the chocolate mixture, cover and refrigerate for a couple of hours until set.

Streusel

⅔ cup packed brown sugar
⅔ cup white sugar
3½ cups all-purpose flour
1½ cups unsalted butter, cut into
  small cubes and chilled

Doughnut dough

1⅔ cups whole milk
1½ Tbsp unsalted butter
3 Tbsp white sugar
1 Tbsp dry active yeast
5½ cups all-purpose flour
2 tsp kosher salt
3 large egg yolks
canola oil for deep-frying

Rosewater glaze

2 Tbsp rosewater
1 cup icing sugar

Streusel Preheat the oven to 350°F. Line a baking sheet with parchment paper.

In the bowl of a stand mixer fitted with a paddle attachment, mix the brown and white sugars and the flour until well combined. Add the butter and combine at medium speed until the mixture becomes a fine crumb (do not overmix or the streusel will become pasty).

Spread the crumbs on the baking sheet and bake, stirring every 6 minutes until golden, about 20 minutes total. Remove from the oven and allow to cool. (If you prefer finer crumbs, pulse them in a food processor.) Will keep in an airtight container at room temperature for up to 10 days.

Doughnut dough Heat the milk and butter in a small pot over medium heat until the butter melts. In the bowl of a stand mixer, combine the warm milk mixture, sugar and yeast until just combined and then set aside the mixture to allow it to activate. Fit the stand mixer with a dough hook. Once the mixture starts to bubble, about 8 minutes, pour in the flour first, followed by the salt and egg yolks. Start the mixer at low speed, and then once the ingredients are combined, increase the speed to medium and continue mixing until the sides of the bowl are clean and the dough is uniform and soft, about 10 minutes.

Turn the dough out onto a clean work surface and knead it about 4 quarter turns until it is nice and tight and smooth on top. Place it in a clean bowl, cover with plastic wrap and allow to rise for about 20 minutes until doubled in size.

recipe continued overleaf…

Roll the dough until it is about 1 inch thick. Using a cookie cutter or a glass, cut out 1-inch rounds and place them on a wire rack. Cover with plastic wrap and allow to proof for another 15 to 20 minutes.

While the dough is proofing, preheat a deep fryer to 350°F. If you don't have a deep fryer, use a large, wide deep-sided pot filled with 4 inches of oil. Heat to 350°F, checking the temperature with a deep-fry thermometer. Line a plate with paper towels. Drop the rounds of dough into the fryer (or pot) and cook, turning them gently with a slotted spoon, for 1 minute or until golden. Transfer the cooked beignets to the paper towel–lined plate to cool.

Rosewater glaze Whisk together the rosewater and icing sugar and set aside. Will keep refrigerated in an airtight container for up to 30 days.

To assemble Scoop the chocolate mousse into a piping bag with a small round tip. Place the rosewater glaze in a small shallow bowl.

Take your cooled beignets and white chocolate mousse piping bag and fill them by inserting the tip of the piping bag into the side of each beignet. Don't be shy. Once the beignets have been filled, dip the top half of each one in the glaze, then top with streusel.

Pie crust

½ cup unsalted butter, cut in small dice

½ cup vegetable shortening, cut into small pieces

3 large eggs

1 cup + ¼ cup water

1 tsp cider vinegar

5⅓ cups all-purpose flour

2 Tbsp kosher salt

1 large egg yolk

8 cups canola oil for deep-frying (optional)

Apple filling

12 cups diced peeled apples (we use McIntosh and Gala)

¾ cup white sugar

3 Tbsp all-purpose flour

1 tsp ground cinnamon

Serves 12 (makes 12 pies)

Apple Hand Pies

A hand pie is an easy-to-make, ever-so-versatile pocket of pie, like a pizza pocket but made of pastry. This version is made with apples, but for an even easier filling, use whichever jam you have in the fridge and add some fresh fruit (use half jam and half fresh fruit), and you will have seasonal hand pies all the time! Warm the jam to melt it a little, add the fresh fruit and allow the mixture to cool, and then continue with the recipe below.

You can make hand pies in any shape you like, from ravioli to half moons or triangles—or impress your friends by doing them different ways. We use half moons here because they're the easiest and their simplicity is beautiful. Once you've baked or deep-fried your hand pies, you can dust the hot pastry with cinnamon sugar, as we do with the apple hand pies at the shop, or with icing sugar, white sugar, demerara sugar. Let your imagination go! Drizzle them with chocolate or vanilla icing . . . the possibilities are endless.

Pie crust Have ready a large square of plastic wrap. Place the butter and shortening together in a bowl and refrigerate until chilled, about 20 minutes.

In a small bowl, whisk together one egg, 1 cup of water and the vinegar and refrigerate.

In a large bowl, combine the flour and salt until well mixed. Add the cold butter and shortening, using your hands to press it into the flour until the mixture resembles coarse crumbs. Make a well in the centre of the flour mixture and add the egg mixture. Using your hands, mix until the dough is just combined. Do not overwork the dough or it will become tough. Form the dough into a ball, wrap it in plastic wrap and refrigerate for 1 hour.

Apple filling Place the apples in a medium pot, add the sugar, flour and cinnamon and mix until the apples are coated. Cook over medium heat for 15 minutes, or until the flour is well absorbed and begins to thicken. Transfer the filling to an airtight container and refrigerate until cool.

Finish pie crust For baked pies, preheat the oven to 350°F and line a baking sheet with parchment paper. (For deep-fried pies, the pies are frozen first, so hold off on preheating the deep fryer.) Have ready a 6-inch round cookie cutter or a small bowl.

In a small bowl, whisk together 2 eggs, the egg yolk and the ¼ cup of water to make an egg wash. Set aside.

Lightly dust a clean work surface with flour. Unwrap the chilled dough, set it on the work surface and roll it into a circle ⅛ inch thick. Using the cookie cutter (or a small bowl), cut out rounds 6 inches in diameter. (You should have 12 rounds.)

Use a pastry brush to brush half of each round with the egg wash. Place a scoop of apple compote on top of the egg wash, leaving ¼ inch between the filling and the edge of the pastry. Fold the unfilled half of the pastry over the filling, matching up the edges and pressing them together with your fingers. Using a fork or your fingers, crimp the edges to seal them and make them decorative. Repeat until all of the pies have been filled and sealed.

To bake the pies, use a sharp knife to pierce a steam hole in the top, set them on the baking sheet and bake for 30 minutes.

To deep-fry the pies, freeze them for a couple of hours before frying.

Preheat a deep fryer to 325°F, or fill a deep-sided pot with 3 inches of canola oil and heat to 325°F (using a deep-fry thermometer to test the temperature). Line a plate with paper towels.

Use a slotted spoon to gently place the pies in the oil and cook for 10 minutes, or until golden. Transfer the cooked pies to the paper towel–lined plate to drain. Serve warm.

Leméac

— *chef* —

MARIE-PIER MORIN

For well over ten years, Restaurant Leméac in Outremont has gained a reputation for exceptional food and professional, European-style service. The brunch and 10pm dinner menus are legendary, but it has a loyal following of celebrities, critics and locals who know that a meal at Leméac—no matter what time of day—will not disappoint. Chef de cuisine Marie-Pier Morin was born into the industry and started as a pastry chef, but she has steadily risen to the top of the food chain and now leads the highly disciplined team that produces Leméac's beloved classics.

We love the charming and elegant space that is one of the few truly French bistros in the city, and the food continues to shine. Marie-Pier has kept up Leméac's standards while introducing new ideas and flavours, such as the snails, portobello and tomato ragoût in basil sauce found on her after-10pm evening menu. It is the perfect spot for après-theatre nights.

facing VEAL SWEETBREADS, CAULIFLOWER PURÉE AND FRIED CAULIFLOWER WITH SHERRY AND HAZELNUT SAUCE

Veal sweetbreads

1¾ lbs veal sweetbreads, soaked
   in water or milk for 2 hours or
   overnight
salt and pepper
2 Tbsp olive oil
¼ cup butter

Sherry and hazelnut sauce

2 Tbsp olive oil
2 Tbsp finely chopped shallots
2 Tbsp sliced carrots
2 Tbsp finely chopped celery
1 garlic clove, minced
2 sprigs fresh thyme

½ cup sherry
¼ cup sherry vinegar
4 cups veal stock
¼ cup toasted hazelnuts,
   peeled and chopped
hazelnut oil for finishing

Veal Sweetbreads, Cauliflower Purée and Fried Cauliflower with Sherry and Hazelnut Sauce

Serves four

Although there are several parts to this dish, none of them is hard to prepare. However, have your plates warmed so you can plate the sweetbreads as soon as the fried cauliflower has been cooked.

Veal sweetbreads Fill a large bowl with ice water.

Bring a large pot of water to a boil over high heat. Add the sweetbreads and blanch for 3 to 4 minutes, then remove from the heat and plunge them into the ice water. Allow to sit until cool enough to handle.

Using a sharp knife, peel off and discard the outer membrane. Using your fingers, pull out the veins from inside the sweetbreads. If they tear a little while pulling out the veins, don't worry. Discard the viscera. Separate the cleaned sweetbreads into 4 pieces, and set them on a plate lined with a tea towel and refrigerate until needed.

Sherry and hazelnut sauce Heat the olive oil in a medium saucepan over medium-high heat. Add the shallots, carrots, celery and garlic and sauté for 2 minutes, or until softened. Stir in the thyme, sherry and vinegar. Reduce the heat to low and simmer until reduced to three-quarters of the original volume, about 5 minutes. Pour in the veal stock and cook until the sauce has reduced and becomes syrupy, 15 to 20 minutes.

Set a fine-mesh sieve over a clean saucepan. Pour the sauce through the sieve and discard any solids. Set aside.

Cauliflower purée and fried florets Break apart the cauliflower, reserving 4 large florets that you will fry just before serving. Roughly chop the rest into pieces for the purée.

Melt the knob of butter in a medium pot over medium-high heat. Add the onions and sauté until translucent, about

Cauliflower purée and
fried florets
1 large cauliflower
¼ cup + a knob of butter
1 small onion, chopped
3 cups water
kosher salt
2 cups canola oil for frying
1 Tbsp fresh lemon juice

Brussels sprouts leaves
4 large Brussels sprouts, trimmed
    to detach the leaves

2 minutes. Stir in the cauliflower, water and a pinch of salt. Bring to a boil, reduce the heat to low and simmer until the cauliflower is tender, 8 to 10 minutes. Drain well.

Place the cauliflower and the ¼ cup of butter in a food processor and purée until smooth. Season to taste with salt, then set aside.

Brussels sprouts leaves Fill a large bowl with ice water. Separate the individual Brussels sprouts leaves.

Fill a small pot with salted water and bring to a boil over high heat. Add the Brussels sprouts and blanch for 30 seconds, then plunge them into the ice water. Drain and set aside.

Finish sweetbreads Season the sweetbreads with salt and pepper. Heat the olive oil in a frying pan over medium heat. Add

the sweetbreads and cook for 5 minutes. Turn them over and cook for 4 minutes more. Add the butter, baste the meat with it and remove from the heat.

Finish cauliflower florets Preheat a deep fryer to 350°F, or heat the canola oil in a deep-sided pot until it reaches 350°F (check the temperature with a deep-fry thermometer). Drop the florets into the hot oil and fry until golden, about 2 minutes. Using tongs, transfer them to a small bowl. Add the lemon juice and the salt.

To serve Arrange a dollop of the cauliflower purée, a portion of sweetbreads and a floret of fried cauliflower on each plate. Drizzle with some of the sauce, sprinkle with the hazelnuts and garnish with a few drops of hazelnut oil. Top with Brussels sprouts leaves.

Baba au rhum

2 cups all-purpose flour
2½ Tbsp dry active yeast
1 vanilla bean, seeds scraped
   and pod discarded
zest of ½ lemon
1½ Tbsp honey
8 large eggs
⅓ cup butter, room temperature

Blackberries in vanilla syrup

2 cups water
1½ cups white sugar
½ vanilla bean, seeds scraped
   and pod discarded
3 cups fresh blackberries

Baba au Rhum with Blackberries in Vanilla Syrup and Whipped Cream

Makes 14 babas

The baba, a yeast cake, is my favourite dessert, which is why it's now on the Leméac menu. It might seem complicated, but really all you need to do is prepare it forty-eight hours ahead. You will need fourteen 4-inch baba moulds (or savarin moulds or ring moulds) and a candy thermometer, but this dessert is so worth it!

Baba au rhum Lightly grease fourteen 4-inch baba moulds with a bit of butter. Place on a baking sheet.

In the bowl of a stand mixer fitted with a paddle attachment, combine the flour, yeast, vanilla, lemon zest, honey and 4 of the eggs. Beat at medium speed until the batter comes away from the sides of the bowl, about 5 minutes.

Add the remaining 4 eggs and beat again until the batter again comes away from the sides. Gradually add the butter, beating constantly, then beat for another 2 minutes. Cover the mixing bowl with a clean cloth and allow the mixture to sit for 20 minutes.

Divide the batter among the moulds. Cover with a clean cloth and allow to sit for 20 minutes.

Preheat the oven to 350°F. Place the babas on the centre rack and bake for 15 minutes. Transfer them to a wire rack to cool slightly, then tap the babas out of their moulds and allow them to dry on the rack for 48 hours.

Blackberries in vanilla syrup Place the water, sugar and vanilla in a small pot and bring to a boil over medium heat. Remove from the heat and allow to sit for 5 minutes.

Rum syrup

6 cups water

7 cups icing sugar

zest of 1 lemon

zest of 1 orange

2 vanilla beans, seeds scraped
   and pods discarded

1½ cups dark rum

Sweetened whipped cream

2 cups whipping cream

3 Tbsp icing sugar

1 vanilla bean, seeds scraped
   and pod discarded

Place the blackberries in a medium nonreactive bowl. Pour the hot syrup over the fruit and allow to cool to room temperature. Refrigerate.

Rum syrup In a large pot, bring the water, icing sugar, lemon and orange zests and the vanilla to a boil over medium-high heat. Remove from the heat and stir in the rum. Allow the syrup to cool to 140°F (use a thermometer to test the temperature).

Set a wire rack over a large plate. Submerge the babas in the syrup, in batches, if necessary, until they are soaked through, then transfer them to the wire rack to drain. Will keep refrigerated in an airtight container for 10 days.

Sweetened whipped cream In the bowl of a stand mixer fitted with a whip attachment, combine the cream, sugar and vanilla and beat at high speed until you achieve the desired consistency.

To serve Remove the babas from the fridge and allow them to come to room temperature. Arrange a baba on each plate and spoon the blackberries overtop. Garnish with dollops of sweetened whipped cream. Enjoy.

Maison Publique

—— chef ——

DEREK DAMMANN

When we need a night out at a neigh-bourhood pub, we often head to Maison Publique in the Plateau. The northern England–styled pub is set among houses in this residential area, and it's a great place to catch up with friends, strike up a conversation with the staff and sample from an eclectic but accomplished menu.

Chef Derek Dammann is originally from Campbell River, BC, but he spent four years working in England at Jamie Oliver's Fifteen, along with short stints at Fergus Henderson's St. John and Heston Blumenthal's Fat Duck. When his visa ran out, Derek booked a one-way ticket to Montreal and delighted us with his inventive style and culinary prowess at DNA. At Maison Publique, which Derek co-owns with Jamie Oliver, we like to tuck into a warm corner of his forty-seat restaurant or sit at the large, beautiful custom-made wood bar and order his homemade charcuterie (the best in the city!). From there, we can look onto an opening of the kitchen and see what's cooking.

We order from their menu, which features exclusively Canadian ingredients to pair with an extensive list of Canadian wines. We especially like the gnudi with venison ragù and chestnut, bacon and cabbage on wintry nights and the signature hard cider made from Quebec apples. Whatever the season, we feel at home in this cozy, welcoming room where the food is always delicious and ever-changing.

facing SNOW CRAB TART

Pâte brisée

2½ cups all-purpose flour
1¼ tsp kosher salt
1¼ cups unsalted butter, cold,
  cut into ½-inch pieces
5 Tbsp water, ice cold
1 large egg white, lightly beaten

Snow crab filling

3 Tbsp olive oil
1 onion, julienned
3 garlic cloves, minced
1 fresh cayenne (or jalapeño) pepper,
  seeded and finely chopped
1 lb snow crab meat, cooked and
  picked over for shells

1 Tbsp fresh lemon juice
¼ cup finely chopped fresh cilantro
3 Tbsp freshly grated Parmesan
  kosher salt and black pepper to taste
2 large eggs
2 large egg yolks
⅔ cup whipping cream
⅔ cup whole milk

*Serves 8
(makes one
10-inch tart)*

Snow Crab Tart

This recipe breaks the traditional rule that cheese and fish don't mix; here the addition of the Parmesan really brings all the flavours together. You could use any type of crab really, but since our seafood comes from Eastern Canada, snow crab seems the logical choice here. You could also make individual tarts if you wanted, but I find one large one less finicky—and it avoids that drastic pitfall of too much crust and not enough filling. Serve the tart with lemon wedges at room temperature; it really doesn't need anything else.

Pâte brisée Have ready a large piece of plastic wrap. Combine the flour and salt in a large bowl. Add the butter, toss gently to combine and then, working quickly with your fingertips, work the butter into the flour until the pieces are smaller than a pea and evenly distributed.

Drizzle in 3 Tbsp of the ice water and mix until the dough starts to come together when pinched. If the dough still seems a bit dry and crumbly, add the remaining 2 Tbsp water. Using your hands, shape the dough into a 1-inch-thick disc. Wrap the dough tightly in plastic wrap and refrigerate for 2 hours or up to 24 hours. Remove the dough 30 minutes before you plan to roll it, and allow it to come to room temperature.

Lightly dust a clean work surface with flour. Have ready a 10-inch tart shell with a removable bottom, a 10-inch round of parchment paper and some baking weights (or dry beans).

Using a rolling pin lightly dusted with flour, roll out the pastry dough until it is about 12 inches in diameter and about ⅛ inch thick. Roll outward from the centre, rotating the dough and dusting the work surface with flour to prevent sticking. Carefully roll the pastry dough into the tart shell, pressing it against the sides and into the corners gently. Trim any pastry hanging over the edges. Place the tart shell on a baking sheet and refrigerate for 30 minutes.

Preheat the oven to 350°F. Prick the pastry several times with a fork, then cover it with parchment paper and fill with the baking weights (or dry beans). Bake for 12½ minutes, rotate the pan 180 degrees and bake for another 12½ minutes. Remove from the oven and take out the baking weights (or dry beans), then continue to bake for 10 to 12 minutes more, until the pastry begins to become golden. Remove from the oven, and while the shell is still hot, brush the pastry with the egg white to seal it. Set aside to cool, but leave the oven on while you prepare the filling.

Snow crab filling Heat the olive oil in a large frying pan over medium-high heat until it is almost smoking. Add the onions and sauté until they are soft and starting to become golden, about 2 minutes. Stir in the garlic and fresh cayenne (or jalapeño) and sauté for 30 seconds. Remove the pan from the heat and add the crabmeat, tossing gently to combine. Scrape the mixture into a large nonreactive bowl and add the lemon juice, cilantro, Parmesan and salt and pepper. Turn this mixture into the baked pastry shell and smooth the surface gently without pressing down on the filling.

In a medium bowl, whisk together the eggs, egg yolks, cream and milk until well combined. Pour this custard mixture over the crabmeat, making sure that it fills in all the cracks and crevices (reserve any extra custard), then bake the tart for 7 minutes. Open the oven door and carefully pour the remaining custard into the pastry shell so the filling is flush with the crust. Cook for another 20 minutes, then rotate the tart shell 180 degrees and cook for 20 to 25 minutes more. The filling should be firm when you tap the pan. If it ripples, the custard has not set. Cook for another 5 to 10 minutes.

Remove the tart from the oven, transfer to a cooling rack and allow to rest for at least 1 hour before slicing.

Garlic broth

3 cloves garlic, peeled and crushed
   with the back of a knife
1 Tbsp kosher salt
3 fresh sage leaves
1 fresh bay leaf
6 black peppercorns, freshly cracked
4 cups water

Wild garlic purée

1 cup wild garlic (ramps), green
   leaves only
1 cup canola oil
kosher salt

Aigo Bouido
(Garlic Broth with Runny Egg Yolk and a Wild Garlic Crouton)

Serves four

In Provençal dialect, *aigo bouido* means "boiled water." This soup is nothing more than a lightly flavoured garlic broth using Montreal's finest, but when made with care it is an amazing introduction to a meal. Traditionally, it's just the broth, but I like to gild the lily with an egg yolk, a crouton spread with wild garlic purée and a few shavings of really good Avonlea cheddar. Grilling the bread over charcoal provides the perfect rustic touch.

Garlic broth Place all of the ingredients in a heavy-bottomed saucepan and bring to a boil over medium heat. Reduce the heat to low and simmer for 20 minutes, then remove from the heat. Set a fine-mesh sieve over a clean saucepan and strain the broth. Discard the solids.

Wild garlic purée Fill a large bowl with ice water. Fill a second large bowl with ice cubes or crushed ice.

Bring a large pot of salted water to a rolling boil over high heat. Add half of the wild garlic leaves and blanch for 15 seconds. Drain the leaves in a colander and immediately plunge them into the ice water. Drain them again, squeezing out as much of the excess water as possible and set aside.

Garnishes
4 slices sourdough bread
1 garlic clove, peeled and cut in half
flaky sea salt and black pepper
4 large egg yolks
really good-quality olive oil for
    drizzling
Avonlea cheddar

Using a sharp knife, roughly chop the raw and blanched leaves. Place in a blender and purée on high speed for 15 seconds. With the motor running at high speed, add the canola oil in a thin, steady stream until emulsified. Season with salt, scrape the mixture into a small bowl and set it over the ice cubes to cool quickly and help it retain its colour.

Garnishes Preheat a charcoal grill or the oven to 400°F. Place the bread on the grill and toast for 1 to 2 minutes per side. Rub both sides of each bread slice with the cut side of the garlic. Spread each slice of toast with wild garlic purée and season with the flaky salt.

Place the broth over medium-high heat and bring to a simmer. Season with salt and pepper, if necessary.

To serve, drop an egg yolk into the bottom of 4 warmed soup bowls. Pour the hot broth around the egg yolk, and generously drizzle the soup with olive oil. Float the garlic toast in the soup, and garnish with a few shavings of Avonlea cheddar.

Manitoba

—— *chef* ——

CHRISTOPHER PARASIUK

Who knew that a vacant woodshop in Park Ex would become a Montreal culinary legend? When former gardener and herbalist Elisabeth Cardin took over the space in 2013, she first envisioned it as a shared workspace. When that didn't work out, she then reimagined the place as a restaurant serving wild foraged products, local and homemade everything and natural wine. With builder and designer Simon Cantin and Chef Christopher Parasiuk, formerly part of Jason Nelson's team at Renard Artisan Bistro, on board, Elisabeth has realized her vision.

We love the creative and wholly original dishes and the opportunity to learn about edible plants and weeds found in our own backyard. And we're not alone: the restaurant has been drawing a steady stream of curious diners since it opened. Chef Parasiuk brings out the best flavours from his foraged ingredients and pairs them well with his other specialty, the game meats on his menu. All of the ingredients are sourced from local suppliers as well as from Elisabeth's own forays along city streets and gardens and into local forests. Among our favourite dishes are the deer heart gravlax with cauliflower purée, sunflower seeds, apples and fried lichen as well as the spruce blood sausage with molasses bread, clams and squash berries. The menu changes seasonally, which means an ever-changing selection of innovative new dishes to try.

Labneh
½ cup plain yogurt
pinch of salt

Roasted spaghetti squash
1 medium spaghetti squash
1 Tbsp canola oil
2 Tbsp butter
1 tsp smoked paprika
salt and black pepper

Spaghetti Squash, Wild Hedgehog Mushrooms and Brussels Sprouts in Cedar Butter

Serves 4 to 6

Next time you go for a hike in the forest, bring back a couple of small cedar branches. They have larger, flatter leaves than other coniferous trees and have a lovely sweet flavour; this cedar butter (you will have extra) is lovely on toast for your mornings at the cabin. Hedgehog mushrooms can be found at farmers' markets in the summer and fall. They have a nice earthy flavour and go perfectly with coniferous plants. If you are making this dish out of the season or you just can't find any, substitute *maitake* mushrooms, shiitakes or oysters. It's worth making the time to prepare homemade labneh, but if you prefer, you can substitute sour cream instead.

Labneh Line a colander with a clean cloth or a tea towel and set it over a bowl.

Combine the yogurt and salt in a bowl and mix well. Pour it into the cloth-lined colander, cover it with another cloth or tea towel and allow it to sit at room temperature for 12 to 24 hours. Will keep refrigerated in an airtight container for up to 10 days.

Roasted spaghetti squash Preheat the oven to 350°F. Have ready a sheet of parchment paper and a sheet of aluminum foil.

Cut the squash in half lengthwise. Using a spoon, remove and discard the pulp and seeds. Place the squash, cut sides up, on a baking sheet. Drizzle canola oil evenly over the squash, dab them with the butter and sprinkle with smoked paprika and salt and pepper. Cover the squash with the parchment paper and the aluminum foil and roast for 25 to 35 minutes, or until the squash is tender. Remove from the oven and set aside.

Cedar butter
½ cedar branch
½ cup butter, room temperature
salt and black pepper

Glazed vegetables
handful of Brussels sprouts
handful of wild hedgehog mushrooms
(or oyster mushrooms, maitakes or
shiitakes)
2 Tbsp butter
2 Tbsp + a dash of canola oil
2 shallots, sliced

2 Tbsp + a dash of cider
vinegar
1 tsp Worcestershire sauce
1 Tbsp + a dash of maple syrup
1 tsp cedar butter (recipe here),
chilled
1 carrot, julienned
2 Tbsp pumpkin seeds, toasted

Cedar butter Preheat the oven to 375°F. Lightly toast the cedar branch, on a baking sheet, in the oven to release the aromas, about 5 minutes. Remove the cedar branch from the oven, allow it to cool slightly and then pick off the green leaves. Discard the branch or use it in your next meat or veggie stock. Place the leaves in a small coffee grinder and process until you have a coarse powder.

Place the cedar powder in a small bowl and add the butter. Using the back of a fork, work the cedar powder into the butter until it is evenly distributed. Season with salt and pepper. Will keep refrigerated, wrapped in waxed paper, for 2 weeks, or frozen for a month.

Glazed vegetables Trim the bottom off the Brussels sprouts, and cut a small X into the core so that they cook more evenly. Peel the outer leaves from the Brussels sprouts and set them aside.

Fill a large bowl with ice water. Bring a large pot of salted water to a boil over high heat. Add the Brussels sprouts and blanch them for 7 minutes. Using a slotted spoon, immediately transfer the Brussels sprouts to the bowl of ice water to stop the cooking and preserve their colour. Allow them to drain well and then set them aside in a small bowl.

Add the Brussels sprouts leaves to the pot of boiling water and blanch them for 1 minute. Drain well and immediately transfer them to the bowl of ice water to stop the cooking. Drain well and set aside.

Using a spoon, remove the gills from the underside of the mushrooms so they do not burn and become bitter. (Save them for another use, e.g., mix them with lots of salt to make a mushroom salt.) Depending on the size of the mushrooms, tear them into pieces about the same size as the Brussels sprouts. Set aside the mushrooms.

recipe continued overleaf...

Melt the butter and canola oil in a sauté pan over medium-high heat. Add most of the shallots (setting aside a pinch for the Brussels sprouts leaves) and sauté until translucent, about 5 minutes. Stir in the whole Brussels sprouts (not the leaves) and the mushrooms and cook until the mushrooms are tender, about 4 minutes.

Deglaze the pan with the 2 Tbsp of vinegar, then add the Worcestershire sauce and 1 Tbsp of the maple syrup. Whisk in the 1 tsp cedar butter until emulsified. Season as needed with salt and pepper and more maple syrup or Worcestershire sauce. Set aside in a warm place.

In a small bowl, combine the Brussels sprouts leaves and carrots with the reserved pinch of shallots. Add the dashes of vinegar, canola oil and maple syrup and toss well. Season with salt and pepper to taste.

To serve Smear each plate with a spoonful of labneh and set one-quarter of a squash on top. Using a fork scrape the squash but leave it in the skin. Pour the glazed vegetables into the squash, top with the Brussels sprouts, mushrooms and carrots and finish with some toasted pumpkin seeds.

Confit Jerusalem artichokes

2 lbs Jerusalem artichokes (about 10)
6 cups quality sunflower oil
½ garlic clove
5 sprigs fresh balsam fir or thyme
5 sprigs fresh spruce or rosemary
2 sprigs fresh sage

Sunflower butter

1 cup sunflower seeds (shelled,
   but untoasted and unsalted)
2 Tbsp sunflower oil
 salt and black pepper
¼ cup butter
1 tsp maple syrup
1 tsp cider vinegar

Confit Jerusalem Artichokes, Sunflower Seed Butter, Northern Spiced Rum Raisins and Green Bean and Apple Salad

Serves 4 to 6

Jerusalem artichokes are a root vegetable that can be found at most farmers' markets year round. Chic Choc rum is made in Quebec and contains several wild plants native to the region. You can find it at most SAQ liquor stores. Use the balsam fir or spruce if you or someone you know has what is for certain a fir or spruce tree in the backyard; otherwise, using the thyme and rosemary is just fine. Garnish this salad as we do in the restaurant with beet chips and/or toasted sunflower seeds for a little crunch.

Confit Jerusalem artichokes Preheat the oven to 300°F. Have ready some parchment paper and aluminum foil.

Using a scrub brush, wash the artichokes in cold water to remove all of the dirt. Rinse them well. Place the artichokes in a deep roasting pan and cover them with the sunflower oil. Add the garlic, balsam fir (or thyme), spruce leaves (or rosemary) and the sage. Cover the pan with a sheet of parchment paper and then a sheet of foil. Roast for 3 hours, or until the artichokes are tender. Remove from the oven and set aside to cool. Set aside 2 Tbsp of the confit oil for the green bean and apple salad.

Sunflower butter Preheat the oven to 350°F. Line a baking sheet with parchment paper. Place the sunflower seeds and sunflower oil in a small bowl, season with salt and pepper and toss until well combined. Transfer to the baking sheet and bake for 8 to 10 minutes, or until the seeds are lightly toasted.

Transfer the sunflower seeds to a blender or food processor, add the butter,

Marinated raisins

½ cup raisins
1 tsp maple syrup
1 tsp cider vinegar
½ cup Chic Choc rum
salt and black pepper

Green bean and apple salad

1 lb green beans, trimmed
1 Empire apple (or any firm variety)
1 shallot, sliced
1 Tbsp cider vinegar
2 Tbsp reserved sunflower oil (from the confit Jerusalem artichokes)
1 tsp maple syrup
salt and black pepper

maple syrup and vinegar and blitz to a chunky consistency. Will keep refrigerated in an airtight container for 2 to 3 weeks.

Marinated raisins Place all of the ingredients in a small pot over low heat. Cook the mixture slowly, stirring occasionally, until the raisins absorb some of the liquid, about 15 minutes. Remove from the heat and allow the raisins to cool in the liquid. Will keep refrigerated in an airtight container for about 2 weeks.

Green bean and apple salad Fill a large bowl with ice water. Bring a large pot of salted water to a boil over high heat. Add the green beans and blanch them for 7 minutes. Drain the beans and place them immediately in the ice water to stop the cooking and preserve their colour. Drain and set aside.

Slice the apple into bite-sized pieces and place it in a large bowl. Add the green beans, shallots, vinegar, reserved sunflower oil and maple syrup and toss well. Season to taste with salt and pepper and more vinegar and/or maple syrup, as required.

To serve Place a spoonful of the sunflower butter on each plate. Arrange the salad on top, nestle a couple warm Jerusalem artichokes around the salad, and garnish with the raisins.

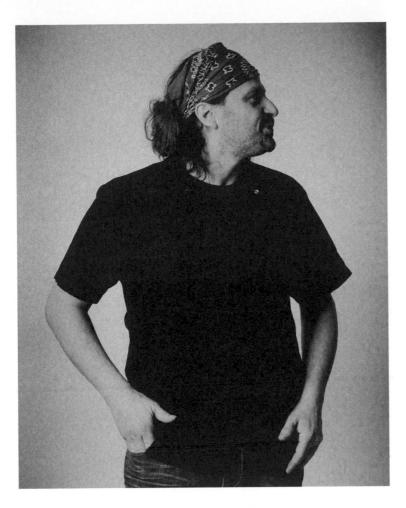

Mercuri
Montréal

—— *chef* ——

JOE MERCURI

When we can't decide between fine dining and sitting around the fire, we go to Mercuri Montréal! A ten-by-five-foot open wood fire pit takes pride of place in one large room of the restaurant while a formal dining room holds court in another, making this Old Montreal gem unique on the Quebec dining scene. We are naturally drawn to the warm, casual atmosphere of the fire pit, which is like sitting around an open hearth. From our bar-height tables, we enjoy unlimited views of Mercuri Montréal's staff tending to the fire, whose burning maple and Binchotan wood flavours many of our foods.

Chef Joe Mercuri made his name at Brontë with signature dishes that creatively combined flavours and textures with beautiful presentation. At Mercuri Montréal, the wide-ranging menu gives Chef Mercuri lots of room to play. We love the tender cornbread with rich, velvety melted cheese and roasted fennel, and a recent barbecued salmon head was a rare treat of crispy skin and smoky aroma. What we like most is that whether we choose the fire pit or the formal dining room, the meal will be an adventure! Here's your chance to bring the full Mercuri experience to your dinner table at home.

Leek ash
1 medium leek, trimmed
1 Tbsp canola oil

Brown butter
60 g unsalted butter

Marinated grilled bell peppers
400 g "ancient sweets" peppers
50 g olive oil
50 g Cabernet vinegar or white
    balsamic vinegar
5 g kosher salt
3 g cracked black pepper
200 g Swiss chard leaves, washed
    and cut into thin strips

Sweet and sour pearl onions
60 g pearl onions, peeled and halved
60 g Cabernet vinegar
45 g honey
40 g chicken stock
20 g cracked black pepper
6 g sriracha

Red Peppers / Feta / Gnocchi / Pearl Onions / Brown Butter

Serves four

Homemade chicken stock will make a big difference to the flavour of the pearl onions in this recipe; simmer some raw chicken bones for two to three hours and make your own. In a pinch, buy a good-quality, low-sodium, organic chicken stock instead. Look for Cabernet vinegar and buffalo milk yogurt at fine foods stores. And seek out the kuzu starch from a Japanese grocery store.

Leek ash Preheat the oven to 450°F. Place the leek on a small baking sheet brushed lightly with some of the oil, then brush the leek as well. Bake for 2 to 3 hours, or until the leek is completely burnt and black.

Allow to cool. Break off the black layers, and process in a coffee grinder until you have a very fine powder. Sift the ash through a fine-mesh strainer into an airtight container. Set aside.

Brown butter Melt the butter in a small saucepan over medium heat, stirring every 5 minutes until it caramelizes and smells nutty, about 20 minutes.

Place a fine-mesh sieve over a clean bowl, strain the brown butter through it and discard the solids. Refrigerate the butter, uncovered, until cool. Set aside.

Marinated grilled bell peppers Preheat a grill or stovetop grill pan to medium-high. Place the bell peppers on the grill and turn them occasionally until the skins are charred, 6 to 8 minutes. Transfer the peppers to a bowl, cover and allow to cool slightly, about 20 minutes.

Peel and discard the charred skins and the seeds. Cut each bell pepper into 6 segments and place in a large bowl. Add the olive oil, vinegar, salt and pepper and toss well to combine. Set aside to marinate for 30 minutes.

Once marinated, gently stir in the Swiss chard until well mixed, and set aside until needed.

Charred pearl onions

1 tsp canola oil

4 pearl onions, peeled and
   cut in half

Gnocchi

200 g whole milk

50 g plain buffalo milk yogurt

3 black peppercorns

3 bay leaves

2 Tbsp olive oil + more for drizzling

2 shallots, finely chopped

65 g white wine

75 g feta cheese

75 g mascarpone cheese

5 g light soy sauce

5 g mirin

5 g kosher salt

pinch of kosher salt

56 g kuzu root starch or cornstarch

56 g whole milk

10 g Parmesan, finely grated

canola oil for deep-frying

½ cup all-purpose flour for dusting

micro greens for garnish

ingredients continued…

Sweet and sour pearl onions Place the pearl onions in a medium pot. Add the remaining ingredients and cook over medium-low heat until the onions are tender and the sauce coats the back of a spoon, about 5 minutes. Set aside.

Charred pearl onions Heat a small sauté pan over medium-high heat, then add the canola oil. Once the pan is very hot, add the pearl onions cut side down. Cook without moving for 8 to 20 minutes, or until the cut side is very dark and charred. Remove and set aside.

Gnocchi Place the 200 g of milk, yogurt, peppercorns and bay leaves into a small pot over medium-low heat. Slowly heat the milk until it is warm to the touch and steam starts to rise, about 10 minutes. Do not bring to a boil or the mixture will split.

Heat the olive oil in a small sauté pan over medium heat. Add the shallots and cook, stirring occasionally until caramelized, about 10 minutes. Pour in the wine and allow to simmer for 10 minutes.

Place a fine-mesh sieve over a clean bowl, strain the shallot-wine mixture through it and discard the solids. Pour the wine mixture into the infused milk. Whisk in the feta cheese, mascarpone, soy sauce, mirin and salt.

Prepare a slurry by combining the kuzu root starch (or cornstarch) with the 56 g of milk in a small bowl until well mixed.

Place the cheese mixture over medium-high heat, stir in the starch slurry and bring to a boil. Reduce the heat to medium, simmer for 40 seconds, whisking constantly, and remove from the heat. Allow to cool to room temperature, then stir in the Parmesan.

Cut three 8 × 16-inch sheets of plastic wrap, and place one of the sheets on a clean work surface. Have ready a large bowl with ice cubes. Scoop the gnocchi

recipe continued overleaf…

Brown butter crumble

50 g all-purpose flour
50 g almond flour
50 g brown sugar
½ pinch kosher salt
50 g brown butter (page 144),
   cut into small cubes

dough into a piping bag with a 13 mm diameter round tip. Pipe a 12-inch-long noodle onto the plastic wrap. Wrap the plastic around the dough very tightly, creating a sausage-like round. Twist the ends until the tube begins to get stiff and the dough inside is compressed slightly, but is still 12 inches long with a 13 mm diameter. Repeat twice with the remaining dough. Place the "sausages" in the bowl of ice, in the fridge, and chill for 1 hour.

Brown butter crumble Preheat the oven to 325°F. Line a baking sheet with parchment paper.

Combine the flours, brown sugar and salt in a medium bowl. Add the brown butter, and using a fork, work the butter into the dry mixture until it resembles corn kernels. Transfer to the baking sheet and cook, stirring every 5 minutes, until the mixture is slightly golden, 20 minutes. Set aside to cool.

Finish gnocchi Preheat a deep fryer to 375°F, or heat the canola oil in a deep-sided, heavy-bottomed pot until it reaches 375°F (use a deep-fry thermometer to test the temperature). Line a large plate with paper towels.

Dust a baking sheet liberally with the flour. Remove and discard the plastic wrap, and cut the gnocchi into 2.5 cm pieces. There should be about 30 pieces. Toss the gnocchi with the flour to coat lightly. Place the gnocchi, just 5 or 6 at a time, into the oil and fry until golden, about 1 minute. Using a slotted spoon, transfer the cooked gnocchi to the paper towel–lined plate to drain.

To serve Divide the marinated grilled peppers and Swiss chard among individual plates. Place 7 to 8 gnocchi on top, and spoon some of the sweet and sour pearl onions, the syrup from the onions and the charred onions around them. Lightly dust the gnocchi with the leek ash. Sprinkle the brown butter crumble around the plate, and drops of olive oil and micro greens on top.

Lemon mostarda

2 Meyer lemons
100 g water
100 g organic white sugar
2 bay leaves
1 star anise
2 g yellow mustard seeds
1 g black mustard seeds
5 g coriander seeds

Salsa verde

35 g fresh parsley
32 g fresh cilantro
25 g fresh mint
20 g fresh basil leaves
10 g fresh tarragon
2 anchovy fillets
10 g capers, drained
100 g extra-virgin olive oil
kosher salt and cracked
   black pepper

White wine shallots

250 g white wine
200 g shallots, cut into thin rings

Garnish

22 g baby fennel
3 g fresh red chili pepper
5 g pine nuts, toasted and roughly
   chopped
3 slices lemon mostarda (recipe here)
2 g fennel fronds
kosher salt to taste
juice of ½ lemon

Tuna / Meyer Lemon / Salsa Verde / Red Chili

Serves four

The leftover lemon *mostarda* makes a great condiment for any roasted or braised meats.

Lemon mostarda Wash and scrub the lemons, then dry well with a tea towel. Using a very sharp knife, slice the lemons about ⅛ inch thick.

Combine the water and sugar in a medium saucepan, and bring to a boil over high heat. Add the bay leaves, star anise, yellow and black mustard seeds, coriander seeds and the lemons and stir to combine. Reduce the heat to medium and simmer for 10 minutes. Turn off the heat and allow the lemons to marinate at room temperature until cool, 1 to 2 hours. Will keep refrigerated in an airtight container for up to 1 month. Bring to room temperature before using.

Salsa verde Place all of the ingredients in a Vitamix or food processor and purée until smooth. Will keep refrigerated in an airtight container for up to 2 days.

White wine shallots Place the wine and shallots in a small saucepan, and cook over medium heat for 5 to 8 minutes, or until the liquid becomes syrupy.

Garnish Using a mandolin, thinly slice the fennel and place it in a bowl. Thinly slice the chilies into rings, discarding the seeds. Add the chilies to the bowl. Stir in the pine nuts, lemon mostarda and fennel fronds and mix well to combine. Season with kosher salt and lemon juice.

Tuna

125 g skinless, boneless sashimi-
   grade yellowfin tuna fillet, cut into
   3 mm slices
8 g Travaglini extra-virgin olive oil
   or another good-quality olive oil
kosher salt
cracked black pepper
syrup from lemon mostarda
   (recipe here)

Tuna Arrange the tuna slices in a single layer on a large plate. Using a pastry brush, brush the tuna on both sides with olive oil and season with salt.

To serve Divide the salsa verde among 4 plates, spreading it into a thin layer. Arrange the tuna slices on top. Garnish with a small amount of the fennel mixture, and place the white wine shallots around. Finish with cracked black pepper, and drizzle a little mostarda syrup around the plate.

Moishes

—— *chef* ——

CARLIN FILLMORE

When we tell friends that we're headed to Moishes for steak, we hear sighs of envy. Seventy-seven years ago, waiter Moishe Lighter won this steakhouse on the Main from his boss in a poker game, and though he was new to the business, he built it into a grand establishment with a reputation for the best steak in the city—and according to *Forbes* magazine, one of the ten best in the world!

Dark narrow stairs lead up to a quiet lounge, where eager diners await their table. The dining room is always bustling with guests remarking on the majestic décor—ballroom light fixtures hanging from pressed-tin ceilings and bare brick walls dressed with large modern paintings—or discussing the fine selections on the wine menu (now presented on iPads) or delighting in their meal.

Chef Carlin Fillmore still serves Moishes' signature coleslaw, dill pickles and Old World favourites such as dry-aged steaks made from locally raised Quebec natural beef. However, he also caters to guests who prefer lighter fare, with such gems as salmon tartare with cucumber and lemon. We can't wait to make this Moishes steak at home!

facing MOISHES' STEAK

Grilled vegetable marinade

2 Tbsp rice vinegar
1 Tbsp minced garlic
pinch of white sugar
1 Tbsp kosher salt
pinch of ground white pepper
1 sprig fresh thyme
¼ cup canola oil
1 small zucchini, cut on the diagonal
   in ½-inch slices
4 spears asparagus, trimmed
1 small red bell pepper, seeded
   and quartered

Charcoal-grilled steak

Quebec charcoal or hardwood
   maple lump charcoal
18 oz rib steak, cut 1 inch thick
kosher salt

Serves one

Moishes' Steak

We cook our steaks over charcoal, so you will need a charcoal grill to do this right. Buy the finest-quality meat you can find, count on an eighteen-ounce steak per person and have a meat thermometer on hand so you do not overcook the meat. Serve your steaks with grilled zucchinis, jumbo red bell peppers and asparagus, and even oyster mushrooms and garlic scapes, flavoured with our grilled vegetable marinade. Prepare the vegetables while the steaks are resting.

Grilled vegetable marinade Pour the rice vinegar into a large bowl. Stir in the garlic, sugar, salt and pepper. Hold the top of the thyme between 2 fingers. Slide the fingers of your other hand down the stem to knock the leaves off. Add the leaves to the vinegar mixture and discard the stems. Using a whisk, slowly incorporate the canola oil until well emulsified. Set aside.

Charcoal-grilled steak Remove the lid and the grill rack from your grill, and add enough charcoal to half-fill it. Remove the steak from the fridge, place on a plate and allow to come to room temperature. Light the grill and wait until most of the coals are burning white and red but the flames have subsided, anywhere from 15 to 25 minutes. Rake the coals around the grill, distributing them evenly across the base of the charcoal grill. Place the grill rack back on and allow it to heat for 3 to 4 minutes.

Immediately season the steak evenly with salt so it has a few minutes to be properly absorbed into the meat. Once the grill rack is hot, place the steak in the most evenly heated area on the grill. We cook the meat for 3 minutes per side for medium rare; however, live charcoal creates its own set of challenges as it is difficult to control the temperature of the grill. So, adjust your cooking time up or down or, better yet, use a meat thermometer to check the internal temperature of the steak. Insert the thermometer parallel to the grill, pushing it through the thickest part of the meat and being careful not to touch the bone. For rare steak, remove the meat from the grill when the thermometer reads 120°F; for medium rare, 125°F; and for medium, 130°F. We do not recommend cooking your meat until it is well done. Transfer the meat to a plate and allow it to rest, uncovered, for 5 minutes.

Finish vegetables To grill the vegetables, make sure your grill is still nice and hot and the charcoal is evenly spread around. Place the zucchini, asparagus and bell peppers directly on the grill rack, and cook them until slightly charred with nice grill marks, 2 to 3 minutes. Using tongs, turn the vegetables over, baste them with the marinade and cook for another 2 to 3 minutes, or until lightly charred. Transfer the cooked vegetables to a plate and baste with a bit more marinade to give them extra flavour and sheen.

To serve Arrange the steak and vegetables on a plate and dig in!

1 Tbsp finely diced shallots

2 Tbsp roughly chopped capers

1 Tbsp finely diced peeled and
    seeded cucumber

½ lemon, finely zested on a rasp

1½ Tbsp fresh lemon juice

2 Tbsp olive oil

8 to 9 oz very fresh organic salmon
    loin, skinless, pin bones removed

1 Tbsp finely chopped fresh chives

salt and white pepper to taste

2 oz fresh horseradish, grated with a
    fine-toothed rasp

1 lemon, cut into wedges

12 to 18 fresh crostini or crackers

Organic Salmon Tartare

Serves 4 to 6

The key to safe and delicious tartare dishes is using the freshest ingredients possible. Ask when the fish came in, and then visually inspect it: it should smell like the ocean, be in one solid piece and look moist (but not slimy). Look for wild salmon (or organic farmed salmon). Refrigerate the salmon at all times, and mix it with the other ingredients just before serving to prevent bacterial growth and spoilage.

—

Combine the shallots, capers and cucumber in a small bowl. Stir in the lemon zest, lemon juice and olive oil until well mixed.

Remove the salmon from the fridge, and clean off and discard any silverskin or stray bones. Using a very sharp knife, mince the salmon and place it in a medium bowl. Pour in the shallot-cucumber mixture, add the chives and mix everything together using a rubber spatula. Season with salt and white pepper.

Mound the salmon tartare in the middle of a large round serving platter, and set the horseradish and lemon wedges alongside. Arrange the crostini or crackers around the tartare. Serve immediately.

Notkins
Oyster Bar

— chef —

DANIEL NOTKIN

We first met Daniel Notkin as he stood at our table describing each of the four varieties of oysters we'd ordered, from their origins to their flavours to which mignonette to use. Our experience with oysters has never been the same since. Owner of the Old Port Fishing Company, which supplies unique oysters to restaurants; champion oyster shucker; founder of the Open Pier Foundation and the popular Montreal Oysterfest; and co-creator of the documentary *Shuckers*, Daniel has single-handedly brought Montrealers together around this humble shellfish.

It comes as no surprise that he's opened an oyster bar on the edge of downtown Montreal, appropriately named Notkins. The large industrial space is sleek and modern with concrete columns, industrial-sized windows, long wooden tables and stainless steel and glass accents. While the space is a far cry from the seashore, Notkins leads a team that turns out platters of the freshest seafood available—from lobster and crab to shrimp, scallops and all the most sustainable products the oceans have to offer. Of course, oysters still take centre stage, whether from as close as Prince Edward Island or as far as New Zealand, whether briny, crisp, sweet or creamy, or with hints of seaweed and minerals.

3 fresh, live lobsters, each 1½ lbs, cold
½ cup table salt (or ½ cup + 2 Tbsp fine sea salt)
2 yellow onions (about ½ lb), skins on, cut into quarters
¾ bottle (341 mL) blond beer
a nice little handful of bay leaves

Steamed Lobsters

Serves three

At Notkins we love lobster. It speaks to us of the end of summer days and early sunset dinners by the beach. But like all seafood, lobster has become a bit of a luxury. So to get the best results for your perfect dinner, read on for a couple of tips for choosing a great lobster and cooking it to perfection.

One of the secrets to great cooked lobster is working quickly and with high heat. Crustaceans contain a lot of enzymes, and these break down and denature the meat quickly between 130°F and 140°F (55°C–60°C), so be sure you've got a big rolling boil and nice hot steam before you start. And a tasty court bouillon will make a flavourful lobster: you can add carrots, lemon and oregano, but I think this nice, reserved recipe is perfect. Serve steamed lobsters with melted butter, freshly baked dinner buns and corn on the cob.

Set the lobsters on the counter (make sure they cannot escape) to come to room temperature while you prepare the court bouillon. Have ready a large stockpot with a tight-fitting lid, a stopwatch (or timer), a heavy-bottomed pot that can go on top of the closed stockpot, and some cloths (to wipe up the court bouillon). You can use a steaming basket if you have one, but it's not necessary.

To make the court bouillon, fill the stockpot with 3 inches of water (use clean ocean water, if possible). Add the salt (if you are not using ocean water), followed by the onions, beer and bay leaves. Cover with the lid and bring to a boil over high heat. Remove the lid and continue to cook at a high rolling boil for 10 minutes to concentrate the flavours in the court bouillon.

When the water is at a rolling boil and the court bouillon has nicely infused, set the steaming basket in the pot (if using) and cover the pot with the lid. Allow the steam in the pot to build for 20 minutes, or until you can see a strong jet of steam escaping. (This pressure will reduce the amount of heat that escapes when adding

recipe continued overleaf…

the lobsters.) Set your stopwatch (or timer) for 7 minutes, 45 seconds, but do not start it.

The extreme heat of the boil is likely to cook the lobster quickly; however, if you have any hesitation, use a heavy knife, place the tip ½ inch behind the eyes on the top centre of the carapace and quickly dash the knife straight down. With the thumb and forefinger of one hand, immediately grab one lobster firmly behind the joints where its claws attach to its body. (There's a good chance it will try to escape unless you've already . . . you know.) With your other hand, quickly lift the lid without releasing too much steam, toss the lobster in and replace the lid immediately. Repeat with the remaining lobsters.

Once all the lobsters are in the pot, start your stopwatch (or timer) and quickly place the heavy pot on top of the lid. This will create a good seal, allowing the steam to build and the water to return much more quickly to the boil (the temperature of the lobsters is lower than the water, so adding 3 of them will reduce the water temperature to well below boiling). Once the water reaches a boil quickly, the court bouillon will splatter and steam out the side of the lid during cooking. It's gonna

get hot in there. Have cloths ready to wipe up the mess.

Have ready a set of tongs and a serving platter. When the timer is up, lift the weight off the lid, remove the lid and, using tongs, transfer the lobsters to the platter.

To serve, have guests tuck napkins into their shirts (or wrap on the bibs), pass around the shell crackers and lobster forks and just start goin'. Afterward, sit back and listen to the waves crashing in the distance.

Picking your lobster Lobsters are live animals, so buy the freshest one you can find—fresh off a fisherman's boat if possible. If not, find a fishmonger you trust, and buy a lobster that's been out of the water for no more than a day.

The other important consideration is whether your lobster is male or female. Why? Females contain roe (roe = eggs), and roe takes longer to cook than lobster meat alone. And you don't want to eat uncooked roe. (Cooked roe, however, is delicious grated over a number of dishes or even the lobster itself, or eaten plain or blended with butter or eggs.) For easy cooking, or if you don't like roe, buy only males. Otherwise, cook your females a little longer—just about forty-five seconds should do it, size depending. (If, when you open the lobster, the roe is still blue, dunk it quickly in the court bouillon to cook it in seconds.) How can you tell whether a lobster is a male or female? Hold the lobster on its back and look at the "swimmerets" (pleopods) along its tail. The ones right at the lobster's midsection are hard for males, soft for females. Additionally, females will have a slight "bulge" on either side. That's right—female lobsters have hips.

Cooking your lobster For years I was a "boiler," reluctant to believe I could impart any flavour to my lobster just by steaming it. But as we looked at different options for the restaurant, I tried steaming. And now it's my go-to method. Why? Basically, with steaming, the heat is consistent (212°F/100°C), and the steam prevents the water molecules in the lobster meat from evaporating, so the lobster remains moist with a natural flavour that tastes a little more . . . "alive" in character. Additionally, it's harder to overcook lobster when it's steamed.

I use 1½-pound lobsters. For me, 1¼ pounds is too small and over two pounds is getting too big. We do not use larger lobsters when cooking at the restaurant because lobsters do not age—all their cells are perfectly reproduced during replication and repair—and as a result, bigger and older lobsters have an even greater reproduction capacity. So we like to keep the big producers around . . .

Classic mignonette (yields 1 cup)
¼ cup finely diced shallots
½ tsp freshly ground black pepper
1 cup good-quality champagne
    vinegar

Spicy vinegar (yields ¾ cup)
¾ cup tarragon vinegar
1 habanero pepper

Each recipe makes enough for about 50 oysters

Raw Oysters with Classic Mignonette and Spicy Vinegar

Oysters. What can we say about oysters that hasn't been said already? They're fantastic, they're odd, they're terrible. Truth is, history is littered with the love of oysters, from contemporary New York City urbanites to the very earliest *Homo sapiens* who were eating shellfish 140,000 years ago. But! The oyster has its fair share of detractors, many misguidedly so. I get about ten people a week who say they don't eat oysters. I ask why . . . and then I suggest they try one with me. Ninety per cent of them go on to become oyster lovers.

The now-classic mignonette is a modern French creation of red wine vinegar, a dice of shallots and ground pepper that balances out the more pronounced flavours of the European flat oysters and the now France-ified *C. gigas* (both have strong seaweed flavours, and potentially high minerality). At the restaurant we serve predominantly East Coast oysters, which have a lighter character, and so we use champagne vinegar in our mignonettes because its delicate complexity and sweetness allow the flavour of these oysters to shine through.

Classic mignonette Combine all of the ingredients in a small bowl or jar. Serve immediately or, for a great comparison, allow to sit for 1 to 2 days until the shallots caramelize and add a little more dark sweetness to the mignonette. To serve, use a small fork or spoon to scoop some of the shallots (leave the liquid behind) into a small mound on the oyster. You want a beautiful little crunch of texture and just a hint of the vinegar.

Spicy vinegar Pour the vinegar into a small bowl. Trim the top of the habanero, removing and discarding the stem but reserving the seeds. Slice the habanero into thin ribbons, place them and the seeds in the vinegar and allow to sit for about 1 hour. The pepper will infuse the vinegar with some heat and negate much of its licorice flavour.

To serve, spoon about half an espresso spoonful of the liquid over the oyster. You want a light nap of liquid heat without any need of texture.

There are two components to falling in love with an oyster: a) choosing a healthy, great, flavourful oyster and b) shucking it properly.

Picking your oyster There are two important considerations when choosing an oyster: its "season" and its harvest date.

People ask me if it's still true that certain months are better. To them I say, "I've never met an oyster that can read a calendar." Oysters only know water temperature. If it's less than 40°F (4°C), they'll "clam up" and consume only the fat and sugar they have stored up over the fall in order to survive the cold. So that means that if we've had a long winter, when the spring thaw comes, a lot of these oysters could have died in hibernation. But even for those surviving oysters, they have to start to feed right away and put their effort into spring/summer reproduction, which makes them thinner and vulnerable again. Remember, though, that the Northern and Southern Hemispheres have opposite seasons, so there's always a beautiful oyster somewhere . . . And given the different seasons and water and temperatures, your favourite oysters this year may be different next year. Oysters can change as continually as the rainfall and weather.

The harvest date is the day that the oyster was taken out of the water. This is

the hallmark of freshness as best it can be measured.

Well, shucks! You've picked a great oyster. Now what? A well-shucked oyster should have the shells open and the oyster released from the shells without damaging the meat, leaving the oyster exposed and free to eat but looking as it did in the shell prior to being shucked: untouched, unscathed and perfect. The reason is this: there are different parts to an oyster, and each part has a different characteristic. When you eat a well-shucked oyster, with each bite you pass through a different part of the oyster. The flavours might start with ocean water and proceed through seagrass and sweetness and vegetal stock, and continue with a beautiful lingering aftertaste.

Opening your oyster Take comfort that many others have been very successful at this task and you can be too. An oyster is attached to its shell by an adductor muscle, a single muscle that attaches it to both the top and bottom shells. Sever this muscle from both shells and the oyster goes free.

A good oyster knife is important. Look for a knife with a relatively fine point (not blunt, though most are so you don't hurt yourself) and a handle that feels good in your hand. All oyster knives will open oysters. I do not encourage the use of real knives or screwdrivers for this purpose, as I have a great many good friends who have stories of emergency rooms and stitches. Oh, and you'll also need a clean cloth about one foot long.

Place the oyster on the cloth nearer to the right side if you are right-handed (and left if you are left-handed), with the hinge toward your shucking hand. Fold the cloth over the oyster, and then place your non-shucking hand firmly on top of the cloth and the oyster beneath to hold it firmly in place. Now fold the last one-third of the cloth back over your hand to protect it from any knife slippage. (You should have a beautiful reverse "S" of cloth curving around the oyster and your hand. You're protected. Mostly.)

Hold the knife firmly and work it into the hinge of the oyster at a forty-five-degree angle. To find the sweet spot, push the knife into the hinge, slowly and with the same force as sharpening a pencil, and roll your knife very gently: roll your wrist forward about ¼ inch, then back ¼ inch—like revving a motorcycle—to wedge the knife in farther. Once the knife is in, it will stand up on its own. Perfection achieved.

At this point, you can remove the cloth. Pry the oyster open with a full twist of the wrist so that your knife is at a ninety-degree angle to the shell. Hold the shells apart with your thumb on one side and your forefinger on the other. Once you have the shells pried open, and your fingers holding them apart, take your knife out and reposition it. Angling the knife at a thirty-degree angle, place it along the top of the shell at the farthest point from you and scrape the top of the shell toward you. (Think of it as scraping the muscle from the top of the shell, like scraping off paint, rather than cutting the oyster open.) Once you have severed the top adductor muscle from the shell, it should just come right off. Check for any fragments of shell under the hinge of the oyster. Turn the oyster toward you, hold it firm and scrape against the shell beneath the oyster to sever the bottom muscle. Now your oyster is ready to eat!

An oyster is an amazing playground for so many flavours. And if you order a dozen, you've got a dozen chances to play. My suggestion is to always try the first oyster without anything. If you've got a great oyster, you'll taste any number of characteristics. So what can complement it? The classic accompaniment to an oyster is a mignonette. Its origins are vague, but today it is—most often—a vinegar-based liquid with shallots and a little ground pepper or any variation thereof. The key is making one that does not overpower the oyster.

Nouveau Palais

—— *chef* ——

GITA SEATON

It was a happy accident that brought together Mary Martha Campbell, a former baker; Jacques Séguin of Raoul's in New York City; and Chef Gita Seaton, originally from Perth, Ontario, to breathe new life into a former seventies-style diner in Mile End. They kept the original décor and the diner's name, Nouveau Palais. They have created an accessible and affordable menu, which features traditional diner items such as mac and cheese, Greek salad and their legendary house burger called #365 burger, named after the overnight bus that rides along Park Avenue. Chef Gita's dishes are well-executed classic comfort food made from well-sourced ingredients.

After completing culinary school, Gita honed her skills in Barcelona with Carles Abellán and locally at Réservoir with Mehdi Brunet-Benkritly and at Le Club Chasse et Pêche with Claude Pelletier. At Nouveau Palais, she's created an atmosphere that's unintimidating, community focused and music driven (many of the staff also work in the music industry). We really enjoy the special DJ nights as well as just eating high-quality yet unpretentious food in a relaxed room with music beats and a good glass of wine. On occasion, the kitchen is open to receiving other chefs who test their own menus on Gita's dedicated followers. We love that she supports her peers by creating a community in her palace. Cheers to Gita!

facing GRILLED HANGER STEAKS AND TZIMMES

Brined hanger steak

5 cups water
¼ cup kosher salt
⅓ cup white sugar
1 bouquet garni (bay leaf, black peppercorn, fresh thyme, garlic, parsley stem)
2 lbs cleaned hanger steak
1 Tbsp canola oil
freshly ground black pepper

Tzimmes

12 fingerling potatoes
1 to 2 delicata squash, washed well but unpeeled
2 Tbsp duck fat
1 cup veal reduction
2 Tbsp maple syrup
2 tsp dry balsam fir needles (or fresh rosemary if you cannot find balsam)
12 pitted prunes
salt and black pepper
pomegranate molasses for drizzling
¼ cup pomegranate seeds for garnish

Grilled Hanger Steaks and Tzimmes

Serves four

Tzimmes is a classic Ashkenazi Jewish dish. More often than not this sweet vegetable stew is made mostly with carrots, but it can also include dried fruit and other root vegetables. Instead of cinnamon, which is commonly found in this stew, we use dried balsam fir. Balsam is a specialty product and can be hard to find, though it can easily be replaced by rosemary.

Brined hanger steak Mix the water, salt and sugar in a large bowl until dissolved. Add the bouquet garni and refrigerate for 12 to 24 hours to allow the flavours to infuse. (Think of it as salty iced tea.)

Cut the hanger steak into 4 equal parts, submerge them in the brine and refrigerate for 1½ hours.

Remove the steak from the brine and pat it dry with paper towels. Discard the brine. Place the steak on a large plate, drizzle with the canola oil and season with some freshly ground pepper.

Tzimmes Bring a medium pot of salted water to a boil over high heat. Add the fingerlings and allow them to cook until tender, 7 to 10 minutes. Remove from the heat, drain and allow to cool completely before cutting them in half lengthwise.

Cut the squash into rounds ½ and ¾ inch thick, and place them in a steaming basket. Bring a pot of water to a boil over high heat, set the squash over the boiling water, cover and steam for 5 to 7 minutes, until tender but not falling apart. Remove from the heat and set aside.

Preheat the oven to 200°F. Line a plate with paper towels. Heat the duck fat in a frying pan over high heat until it is almost smoking. Place the fingerlings, cut side down, in the pan and cook until they are golden (reduce the temperature if the fat starts to burn), about 5 minutes. Transfer the potatoes to the paper towel–lined plate to drain. Place the potatoes in the oven to keep warm.

Return the frying pan to the stove and add the veal reduction, maple syrup and balsam fir (or rosemary) over medium heat. Bring to a simmer and then take off the heat, allowing the mixture to stand for 3 to 4 minutes.

Place a fine-mesh sieve over a clean saucepan and strain the stock mixture through it. Stir in the prunes and the steamed squash. Place the saucepan over medium heat, shaking it gently to emulsify the fats, and allow the sauce to reduce until it lightly coats the back of a spoon, about 3 minutes. Season with salt and black pepper to taste.

Finish steaks Preheat a barbecue to medium heat. Place the steaks on the grill and cook on all sides until they are cooked to your preferred doneness (about 3 minutes per side for medium rare). Remove from the heat and allow to rest for 3 minutes before serving.

To serve, divide the fingerlings and the squash evenly among 4 plates. Spoon some of the tzimmes sauce over the vegetables. Top with a piece of hanger steak and drizzle with pomegranate molasses. Garnish with a few fresh pomegranate seeds and serve immediately.

2 Tbsp blanched spinach

1 bunch fresh basil + a few small
leaves for garnish

salt and black pepper

¾ cup water

3 Tbsp whipping cream

3 large eggs

2 ½ cups all-purpose flour

1 Tbsp chopped fresh parsley

1 cup canola oil + a bit more for
the spätzle

½ head cauliflower, separated
into florets

½ cup vegetable stock (or water)

½ cup butter

¼ cup blanched leeks

½ cup grated Parmesan

24 to 30 pistachios, shelled and
peeled

¼ Granny Smith apple, very thinly
sliced

1 Tbsp good-quality olive oil

fleur de sel for garnish

Cauliflower Spätzle

Serves 4 to 6

Spätzle is an egg noodle common in Eastern European cuisine. Often it is served as a side dish to meats and traditionally it is pan-fried. It is also used in soups. At Nouveau Palais we treat it slightly differently and serve it as a vegetarian main dish. We serve it more like a risotto, with tons of vegetables, buttery sauce and Parmesan cheese. You can prepare the spätzle dough up to two days ahead and assemble this dish at the last minute.

Place the spinach, half of the basil and a pinch of salt in a food processor and purée at high speed until smooth. Gently incorporate the water, cream and eggs.

Place the flour and chopped parsley into a large bowl, making a well in the middle. Pour the spinach mixture into the well, and using a pastry blender, work the wet ingredients into the dry ones until you have a smooth, homogenous dough.

Have ready a colander with holes about ½ inch in diameter. Bring a large pot of salted water to a boil over high heat. Hold the colander directly over the pot and press one-third of the dough through it into the boiling water. Cook until the spätzle floats to the surface, then use a slotted spoon to transfer it to a large bowl. Drizzle the cooked spätzle with a little canola oil and toss gently so it doesn't stick together. Repeat with the remaining dough, in 2 batches, until all the spätzle has been cooked. Set aside. (Cooked spätzle will keep refrigerated in an airtight container for up to 2 days.)

Line a plate with paper towels. Heat the 1 cup canola oil in a frying pan over high heat until it is almost smoking. Add the cauliflower and cook until golden, about 3 minutes. Remove from the heat, transfer the cauliflower to the paper towel–lined plate and allow it to drain.

Roughly chop the remaining basil, reserving a few small leaves for garnish. In a large, clean sauté pan, heat the vegetable stock (or water), ¼ cup of the butter, the cooked spätzle, the leeks and the cauliflower over medium heat, quickly shaking the pan to encourage emulsification. (The sauce should look a bit like a risotto: starchy, buttery, delicious.) Remove the pan from the heat and add the remaining butter, Parmesan, pistachios and chopped basil. Season with salt and pepper to taste.

To serve, spoon the mixture evenly into individual warmed bowls. Garnish with the very thin slices of apple, olive oil, a few small basil leaves and fleur de sel. Serve immediately.

Olive + Gourmando

—— *chef* ——

DYAN SOLOMON

Dyan Solomon's first job in a professional kitchen, at age fifteen, was working for a group of women at a small catering company. The vegetables came from local farms, the freshly baked cookies were made with French chocolate and everything was assembled at a large communal table. She continued to bake and work in restaurants, and she travelled, ran her own business and studied at McGill and then at the New England Culinary Institute in Vermont. Fast-forward fifteen years, and back in Montreal she worked as head pastry chef at Toqué! where she met her business partner, Eric Girard, who was making the bread. Together they now own Olive + Gourmando, a high-end neighbourhood café.

You can take your coffee and pastries to go, but we often end up staying. The communal high tables are great for people-watching and for eyeing the dishes coming from the kitchen. Invariably we end up ordering at least one of the sandwiches, just so we can taste Eric's freshly baked breads. Then we might sample a brioche, like the famous chocolate-banana brioche, and their fragrant soups are hard to resist. To get the full Olive + Gourmando experience, we sometimes clear our schedule and progress from breakfast to lunch and dessert (try the brownies!), happily whiling away a few hours in good company.

¾ cup whipping cream

1½ Tbsp coarsely ground espresso coffee beans (seems like a lot; it's not!)

2½ cups chopped Valrhona dark chocolate (70% cocoa)

1½ cups unsalted butter, room temperature, cut into cubes

1¼ cups chopped Valrhona dark chocolate (70% cocoa)

1¾ cups chopped Callebaut dark chocolate (54.5% cocoa)

6 large eggs, room temperature

1½ cups white sugar

2 tsp vanilla extract

1 cup all-purpose flour

1½ tsp kosher salt

Serves 12 to 24 (depending on how large you want your brownies to be)

Olive's Espresso Brownies

It would be impossible to talk about Olive and not mention our brownies, which are by far our bestselling treat. To inject the flavour of coffee into the brownie, I made a sort of homemade coffee-chocolate chip. It took weeks to get it right so that the coffee ganache wouldn't melt away during the baking, but, oh boy, it was worth it! At the café, we refrigerate the brownies overnight to give them a dense, fudge-like texture—but serve them warm from the oven, if you prefer. Either way is delicious!

Espresso ganache Line a 10 × 15-inch baking sheet with a 1-inch rim with parchment paper.

Place the cream and espresso beans in a small saucepan, and bring to a boil over medium-high heat. Remove from the heat and allow to steep for 5 minutes. Set aside.

Melt the chocolate in a large stainless steel bowl set over a pot of simmering water. Remove the bowl from the pot. Holding a fine-mesh sieve in one hand, carefully pour the infused cream through the sieve directly into the bowl of warm chocolate. Use a rubber spatula to squeeze all the cream from the coffee grinds, try hard not to waste any of this precious liquid. Discard the grinds.

Working quickly, combine the cream and chocolate with the rubber spatula (this step will feel awkward, but it is normal that the chocolate appears granular and feels firm). Spread the ganache onto the baking sheet, trying hard to reach each corner of the pan to create a flat, rectangular shape. Don't worry if it's not perfect; you will be chopping this ganache into small pieces later. Refrigerate until firm, about 30 minutes.

Brownies Preheat the oven to 350°F. Lightly grease and line a 9 × 13-inch pan. Remove the ganache from the fridge and cut it into ½-inch cubes. Set aside.

Melt the Valrhona and Callebaut chocolates and butter in a large stainless steel bowl set over a pot of simmering water, stirring often with a rubber spatula to combine. Turn off the heat and allow the bowl to sit over the warm water.

In the bowl of a stand mixer fitted with a whisk attachment, beat the eggs, sugar and vanilla until light yellow and very smooth, about 5 minutes.

In a small stainless steel bowl, combine the flour and salt and set aside.

Slowly add some of the melted chocolate mixture to the beaten eggs to temper them. Using a wide rubber spatula, fold in the remaining melted chocolate, making sure it is completely combined. In 3 parts, sift the flour mixture directly into the batter, carefully and completely folding it in after each addition. Fold in the ganache cubes and combine well. The batter should look uniform, with no swirls of chocolate; however, try not to overmix it.

Have a kitchen timer ready. Scrape the batter into the pan and bake for 9 to 10 minutes. Turn the pan 180 degrees and bake for another 9 to 14 minutes. If you are using a convection oven, the total cooking time is about 18 minutes. If you are using a non-convection oven, it could take up to 24 minutes. Watch the time carefully and remove the brownie promptly. Gently shake the pan: the brownie should be set (no wobbling in the middle) and uniform in colour (no darkness along the edges). Set the pan on a wire rack and allow to cool for 1 hour.

If you want a traditional light and chewy brownie, release the brownie by gently tugging up on the parchment paper. Remove the brownie from the pan and cut and serve right away. If you want an Olive + Gourmando–style brownie, allow the brownie to cool to room temperature in the pan and then cover with aluminum foil and refrigerate the entire pan overnight. Release and cut the brownies the next day. Allow cut brownies to sit for about 30 minutes to give them a dense, silky and fudgy texture. The best!

2 skinless, boneless organic chicken breasts
extra-virgin olive oil
2 garlic cloves, minced
salt and freshly cracked black pepper
1 cup shelled fresh peas, room temperature
1 cup finely chopped fresh mint leaves
10 cups homemade chicken stock

3 Tbsp unsalted butter
juice of 1 lemon
1½ tsp sea salt for the chicken stock
¼ package (1 lb bag) of best-quality spaghettini, broken into bite-sized pieces
2 cups finely grated aged Pecorino cheese

Best Chicken Noodle Soup Ever

Serves 4 to 6

Soups are special at Olive. We put a lot of effort into our soups, because frankly, soup is one of my favourite things to eat. I love it when a surprising garnish elevates a simple soup and alters our preconceived ideas about what that soup should taste like.

Preheat the oven to 375°F. In a shallow roasting pan, drizzle the chicken breasts generously with olive oil and toss to coat them completely. Add the garlic, and season with salt and pepper. Roast the chicken for 15 to 20 minutes until just cooked through. Allow to cool slightly, then shred by hand and set aside (do not refrigerate).

In a bowl, toss the peas with the mint, and season with a bit of salt. Set aside.

In a large pot, bring the chicken stock, butter, lemon juice and the 1½ tsp salt to a boil over high heat. Reduce the heat to low and simmer for 5 minutes (season with more salt, if needed). Add the pasta and cook until it is *almost* al dente. Stir in the shredded chicken and finish cooking the pasta. Remove the pot from the heat.

To serve, ladle the soup into individual bowls, then garnish with a generous spoonful of the pea-mint mixture, some Pecorino cheese, a drizzle of olive oil and lots of cracked pepper. Serve immediately.

Park Restaurant

—— *chef* ——

ANTONIO PARK

Like many young chefs, Antonio Park first learned about cooking from his mother. She prepared everything from scratch, picking the ingredients fresh daily from the family's one-acre backyard and then drying and milling her own spices, fermenting her own miso and creating her own soy sauce. When the family moved from South America to Montreal, he then worked in his sister's Japanese restaurants before heading overseas to study with several masters at the Michiba culinary school in Japan.

With kimchi and sashimi running through his veins, Antonio delivers some of the best Asian food in the city from his eponymous Westmount restaurant. At the sushi bar, he turns out impeccably prepared sushi, sashimi and other fish dishes inspired by his South American and Korean heritage and his Japanese training. True to his roots, he's meticulous about his ingredients. The soy sauce, rice vinegar and wasabi are homemade, and he is one of the few chefs in Canada to have his own private fish import licence. He also emphasizes healthy spins on traditional dishes by using brown rice, quinoa, organic vegetables and vegan ingredients. The ultimate treat is Park's *omakase*, a chef's choice tasting menu, but all of his dishes are delicious.

facing SALMON OSHIZUSHI

Sushi rice

2 cups Calrose sushi rice or
   Koshihikari short-grain rice
2 cups water
1 cup rice vinegar
¼ cup maple syrup
½ tsp kosher salt
3-inch square of kombu seaweed
4 sheets of nori

Salmon tartare

1 tsp wasabi paste
1 tsp white miso paste
1 tsp kimuchinomoto or kimchi juice
1 tsp honey
1 tsp sesame oil
1 Tbsp sriracha
½ cup peach yogurt (or plain)
¾ cup Japanese Kewpie mayonnaise
   or regular mayonnaise

1 small shallot, finely diced
2 Tbsp chopped fresh chives
12 oz skinless, boneless wild
   (or organic farmed) salmon fillet
   (or sustainable tuna fillet), cut in
   small dice
salt and black pepper to taste
micro greens for garnish

Serves 4 to 6

Salmon (or Tuna) Oshizushi

Impress your guests with this fish tartare with a twist served on top of pressed sushi rice. Oshizushi is made by pressing sushi rice in a special box mould that creates perfect rectangles. Chef Park recommends using a rice cooker and an eight- by three-inch wooden box for this recipe; look for these cookers and three-piece moulds online or in Japanese grocery stores. *Kimuchinomoto* is a Japanese product, a liquid base that can be used to make instant kimchi, the spicy pickle that is a staple of Korean cuisine. It's available at good Asian grocery stores. Although this recipe uses wild salmon or sustainable tuna, use any firm fresh fish of your liking.

Sushi rice Place the rice into the bowl of a rice cooker. Rinse the rice under cold running water until the water runs clear. Drain and add the 2 cups of water. Set

the bowl inside the rice cooker, cover and set to cook. Once the rice has finished cooking, allow it to sit, undisturbed, in the rice cooker for at least 20 minutes. This allows the rice to continue steaming and dry up slightly. Do not rush this stage. Keep the rice warm in the rice cooker until needed.

Salmon tartare In a large bowl, combine the wasabi, miso, kimuchinomoto (or kimchi juice), honey, sesame oil, sriracha, yogurt, mayonnaise, shallots and chives until well mixed. Add the salmon (or tuna) and stir gently to combine. Season with salt and pepper to taste. Cover and refrigerate.

Finish sushi rice Place the vinegar, maple syrup, salt and kombu in a small pot over high heat. Bring to a simmer, remove from the heat immediately, cover and allow to steep for 20 minutes. Remove and discard the kombu.

Have ready a damp tea towel. Place the warm rice in a large bowl. Using a large spatula, slowly drizzle the warm vinegar over the rice, gently folding it in. Be gentle; you do not want to break the grains of rice. Once all the vinegar is incorporated, cover with the tea towel and allow the rice to rest for 5 minutes at room temperature.

Gently fold the rice 5 more times to incorporate any vinegar that has fallen to the bottom. Divide the rice into 4 equal amounts.

To assemble Line the sushi box with a sheet of nori, trimming it if necessary so that no nori hangs over the edge. Have ready 4 sheets of plastic wrap.

Using the spatula, scoop one portion of rice into the prepared sushi box, pressing down with the box lid to create a flat, even surface. Spoon one-quarter of the salmon tartare on top of the rice and gently spread it out. Cover the top with plastic wrap and press down firmly with the lid to flatten it out. (You want to compact but not crush the sushi.) Gently lift up the sides of the box to reveal the finished product, and remove the top, leaving the plastic wrap in place. While the sushi is still sitting on the box base, use a very sharp, clean knife to cut the sushi into 6 to 8 pieces. Remove the plastic. Repeat with the remaining rice and fish. Garnish with micro greens and serve 6 to 8 pieces per person.

Monkfish liver torchon

1 lb monkfish liver
12 cups water
½ cup kosher salt
2 ½ cups sake
thumb-sized piece of fresh
   ginger, thinly sliced

1 bunch green onions, cut in half,
   + 2 green onions, thinly sliced,
   for garnish
4 tsp grated daikon
4 tsp grated fresh ginger
1 sheet of nori, snipped into
   matchstick pieces

Ankimo à la Park
(Monkfish Liver Torchon with Ponzu Sauce)

Serves four

Ankimo, or monkfish liver, is not used a lot in North America, but throughout Japan it is considered a delicacy. Ankimo can be found at a good fish store. It has a subtle flavour, but like foie gras, it is rich and buttery. This recipe follows the traditional Japanese method for rolling and steaming the liver, with hints of French technique. Plan to start this recipe a day ahead so the liver has time to soak, steam and set up before serving. Have ready a twelve- by sixteen-inch piece of cheesecloth to roll the torchon and four lengths of kitchen twine to seal it.

Monkfish liver torchon Using a sharp knife, peel and discard the thin membrane, or skin, from the surface of the monkfish liver. Then, using your fingers, peel away and discard any veins you may see. At this point, the liver should have broken into 4 to 5 pieces.

In a large bowl, whisk together the water and salt until dissolved. Place the liver in a medium bowl, cover with 3 cups of the salted water and refrigerate for 30 minutes. Refrigerate the leftover salted water. Drain the liver, cover with 3 cups more of the salted water and refrigerate for another 30 minutes. Repeat the draining and soaking with the remaining salted water, 2 hours in total.

Drain the soaked liver one last time, pat it dry with paper towels and return it to the medium bowl. Add the sake and allow the liver to marinate for exactly 10 minutes. (Marinating it for too long will mellow the flavour of the liver.) Transfer the liver to a plate and reserve the sake.

Arrange the 12 × 16-inch piece of cheesecloth on a clean work surface. Position the liver in the centre, forming it into a cylinder 2 to 2½ inches in diameter. Fold the bottom of the cheesecloth over the liver, tucking it under the meat to create tension and to mould the liver into a cylinder at the same time. Roll up the liver, encasing it in the cheesecloth. Twist both

Ponzu sauce

Ponzu sauce
½ cup water
¼ cup rice vinegar
2 Tbsp fresh lemon juice
¼ cup soy sauce
1 Tbsp maple syrup
1 Tbsp honey
1 Tbsp sake
½ tsp finely grated fresh ginger
¼ tsp toasted sesame oil

ends to create a tight cylinder roughly 2½ inches in diameter and 8 to 10 inches long. Tie each end with a length of kitchen twine, doing your best to keep the torchon tightly encased.

Set a steamer over a large pot. Pour the reserved sake into the pot and top it off with enough water to fill one-quarter of the pot. Set the pot over medium-high heat and allow the water to come to a boil.

Place the thinly sliced ginger and the bunch of halved green onions in the steamer, and place the monkfish liver on top. Steam for 45 minutes. Remove and discard the ginger and green onions. Transfer the liver to a plate and allow it to cool to room temperature, about 1½ hours. Remove and discard the cheesecloth. The liver will still be soft and will fall apart.

Arrange a 12 × 16-inch sheet of plastic wrap on a clean work surface. Place the liver in the centre of the plastic wrap, forming it into a 2 to 2½-inch cylinder, just as you did on the cheesecloth earlier. Fold the bottom of the plastic wrap over the liver, tucking it under the meat. Roll up tightly, ensuring there are no air bubbles. Holding the ends, roll the liver on the counter, like a rolling pin, to create a smoother cylinder. Twist both ends to create a tight cylinder, and tie each end with a length of kitchen twine, doing your best to keep the liver tightly encased. Refrigerate for 12 to 24 hours.

Ponzu sauce Combine all ingredients in a small bowl and whisk together. Will keep refrigerated in an airtight container for up to 5 days.

Finish torchon Remove and discard the plastic wrap from the liver. Using a sharp knife, slice the liver into 1-inch pieces. (You should have about 8 pieces.)

Spoon 4 Tbsp of the ponzu sauce into the bottom of each shallow bowl. Arrange 2 slices of the liver on top and garnish with a teaspoonful each of the grated daikon and ginger. Finish with a sprinkle of the nori and sliced green onions. Serve immediately.

Pastaga

— *chef* —

MARTIN JUNEAU

Pastaga is French slang for *pastis*, the licorice-flavoured apéritif that is so popular in the South of France, and it is a perfect name for a restaurant whose menu features small plates designed to be shared over drinks. Chef Martin Juneau is one of Montreal's most talented chefs: he's apprenticed with Rob Feenie at Lumière in Vancouver and with David Zuddas at Auberge de la Charme in Burgundy and he's run four restaurants of his own, including the highly acclaimed La Montée de Lait. He's won gold among his peers at the national Gold Medal Plates competition, Pastaga has been voted one of the best new restaurants in Canada by *enRoute* magazine and diners like us have been singing his praises since it opened.

For market-fresh Quebec cuisine with a Mediterranean flair and natural organic wines that pair cleverly with the dishes, Pastaga is in a class of its own. We love this casual yet chic restaurant in the Mile-Ex for intimate dinners with friends. The menu changes often depending on what's in season, but we can always count on perfectly executed, creative dishes, like our favourite takes on the quintessential bagel (with chopped liver, onion mousse and pickled red onions) and the crispy maple-glazed pork belly (served on a pancake with pickled carrots).

facing CRISPY MAPLE-GLAZED PORK BELLY, CARROT PANCAKE AND PICKLED CARROTS

2 Tbsp coarse salt
2 Tbsp black peppercorns
2 Tbsp fresh thyme leaves
2 Tbsp minced garlic
2 to 3 lbs pork belly, skin on, in one 8 × 10-inch piece
4 to 6 cups duck fat, melted
¼ cup maple syrup
¼ cup chopped fresh parsley for garnish

4 medium multicoloured carrots, peeled
¼ cup water
¼ cup white wine vinegar
¼ cup light brown sugar

3 large carrots, peeled and cut in large dice
3 large egg whites
⅔ cup all-purpose flour
salt and black pepper to taste
¼ cup olive oil

Crispy Maple-Glazed Pork Belly, Carrot Pancake and Pickled Carrots

Serves six

Start this dish the day before you plan to serve it, so the pork belly has time to cure.

Crispy maple-glazed pork belly In a small bowl, mix together the salt, peppercorns, thyme and garlic. Using your hands, cover the meat with the salt mixture, and rub it over the pork belly. Place the pork belly in a large casserole dish, cover and refrigerate for at least 12 hours, or overnight.

Rinse the pork belly with cold water and pat dry with a paper towel. In a pot large enough to hold the pork belly, heat the duck fat over medium heat until warm but not hot. Add the pork belly, submerging it in the fat, and reduce the heat to low. Cook for 4 hours, checking occasionally with a deep-fry thermometer to ensure the temperature of the duck fat is about 250°F.

Transfer the pork belly to a baking sheet, skin side down, cover lightly with plastic wrap and a second baking sheet and refrigerate until chilled, 2 to 3 hours. (Discard the fat, or strain it through a fine-mesh sieve and refrigerate it in an airtight container indefinitely to use in place of oil for frying potatoes, eggs, meats and any vegetables.)

Pickled carrots Using a mandolin, very thinly slice the carrots lengthwise. Place the carrot slices in a heatproof bowl.

In a small pot, bring the water, vinegar and brown sugar to a boil over high heat. Once the sugar has dissolved, pour the pickling liquid over the carrots. Allow to cool to room temperature.

Carrot pancakes Place the carrots in a medium pot, cover with cold water and bring to a boil over high heat. Reduce the heat to medium and allow to simmer until very soft, 10 to 15 minutes. Drain well.

Transfer the carrots to a food processor and purée until smooth. Scrape the mixture into a large bowl.

Preheat the oven to 350°F.

In a separate bowl, beat the egg whites until they form stiff peaks. Using a rubber spatula, gently fold the egg whites into the carrot purée by scooping from the bottom of the bowl and folding the carrot onto the whites. Continue folding until you see no more white streaks. Add the flour, gently folding it in until fully incorporated. Season with salt and pepper.

Preheat a large ovenproof frying pan over medium heat. Add the olive oil and swirl it around to coat the pan. Pour in enough batter to make six 3-inch pancakes. (You may need to do this in batches.) Cook until browned on one side, then transfer to the oven to bake for about 10 minutes. Remove from the oven, and using a spatula, carefully flip the pancakes. (They are very delicate.) Again over medium heat, cook until browned on the other side, 2 to 3 minutes. Transfer the cooked pancakes to a plate. Continue cooking pancakes until the batter is finished. Set aside or keep warm in the oven at 250°F.

Finish pork belly Cut the chilled pork belly into 6 equal squares.

Preheat a cast-iron frying pan over medium-low heat. Add the pork belly, skin side down, and cook for 20 minutes, or until the skin becomes golden and crispy. Pour in the maple syrup, spoon it over the pork and cook until the syrup becomes sticky and the pork belly is nicely lacquered on the meat side, about 2 minutes.

To serve Place one carrot pancake in the centre of each plate. Top with a piece of pork belly and garnish with pickled carrots and chopped parsley.

¼ cup + ⅓ cup salted butter

10 oz whole chicken livers

salt and black pepper

2 shallots, chopped

4 tsp red wine vinegar

1 Tbsp salted butter

¼ cup brown sugar

2 Spanish onions, thinly sliced

 salt and black pepper

4 bagels, halved and toasted

¼ cup chopped fresh parsley

¼ cup chopped fresh chives

¼ cup chopped fresh dill

2 small red onions, thinly sliced

½ cup water

½ cup red wine vinegar

½ cup packed brown sugar

Chopped Liver Spread, Toasted Bagels with Caramelized Onion Mousse and Marinated Red Onions

Serves four

At the restaurant, we use Montreal-style bagels from Fairmount Bagel, but you can substitute your favourite good-quality bagel.

Chopped liver Melt ¼ cup of the butter in a small saucepan over high heat. Season the chicken livers with salt and pepper, then add to the pan and sauté for 30 seconds per side until firm to the touch. Transfer the cooked livers to a plate.

Stir in the shallots and deglaze the pan with the vinegar. Remove from the heat.

Using a very sharp knife, finely chop the chicken livers. Add the shallot mixture (including the vinegar glaze) and ⅓ cup of butter. Season to taste with salt and pepper, and set aside at room temperature.

Bagels with onion mousse Preheat the oven to 350°F.

Melt the butter in an ovenproof frying pan over high heat. Add the brown sugar, stirring until dissolved. Stir in the onions and cook for 15 minutes, stirring

frequently. Then place the pan in the oven and cook for 20 minutes, or until the onions are caramelized.

Transfer the onions to a blender and purée until smooth. Season to taste with salt and pepper.

Marinated red onions Place the onions in a medium heatproof bowl.

Combine the water, vinegar and brown sugar in small saucepan and bring to a boil over high heat. Pour the pickling liquid over the onions and allow them to cool to room temperature.

To serve Place a large dollop of chopped liver on each plate. Spread each toasted bagel half with some of the caramelized onion mousse, and place 2 halves over the liver. Serve with a generous amount of marinated red onions on the side and a tablespoon each of fresh parsley, chives and dill sprinkled over the liver and bagel.

Patrice Pâtissier

—— chef ——

PATRICE DEMERS

Patrice Demers has left a legacy of chocolate pot de crème and choux pastry in many of Montreal's best restaurants, including Leméac and Les 400 Coups. He's the author of three successful pastry books and the host of TV's *Les desserts de Patrice*, but we head to Patrice Pâtissier in Little Burgundy to sample his latest creations.

We're always drawn to the glass case at the entrance, where the day's desserts are ready to be boxed and taken away. From there we can peek into the kitchen, where Patrice and his team prepare light lunches as well as desserts that showcase seasonal fruits purchased daily at the market just a few blocks away. These confections always flawlessly balance sweetness and acidity; the pastry is reliably rich and buttery yet light and flaky, and the canelés are soft custard on the inside and perfectly caramelized on the outside.

Instead of a quick coffee and treat to go, we usually get caught up in a web of chocolate-inspired desserts, order a cup of coffee and sit down to savour both. Patrice now offers classes in the room next door, or try these recipes for caramelized apple éclairs and maple financiers.

½ cup unsalted butter
1½ cups fine maple sugar
¾ cup finely ground almonds
½ cup buckwheat flour
¼ tsp salt
6 large egg whites
⅓ cup canola oil

Maple Sugar Financiers

Serves eight

Financiers are little almond-flavoured rectangular cakes traditionally served with tea or coffee. Mix the batter early in the day, allow it to rest for a few hours while you do other things and then bake them quickly before serving. These maple ones are gluten-free and flavoured with maple sugar, which is available in health food stores, public food markets and fine food stores.

Place the butter in a large, deep-sided pot over medium heat and cook for 2 or 3 minutes, or until it begins to separate and the solids start to brown. Remove the pot from the heat and allow the butter to cool slightly.

In a large bowl, combine the maple sugar, ground almonds, buckwheat flour and salt until well mixed. Pour the egg whites over the dry ingredients, then whisk well to combine. Slowly add the canola oil and the brown butter, whisking continuously until you have a smooth, uniform batter. Pour the batter into a smaller bowl, cover with plastic wrap and refrigerate for at least 3 hours.

Preheat the oven to 350°F. Grease with butter and lightly dust with flour eight 4 × 2-inch rectangular moulds (or any other size you prefer). Pour the batter into the moulds and bake for 20 to 30 minutes, or until the cakes are golden and a toothpick inserted in the centre comes out clean. Transfer to a wire rack and allow to cool for at least 15 minutes. Invert from the moulds. Financiers are best eaten the same day, at room temperature, to appreciate their almost crispy texture on the outside and their moist and buttery crumb on the inside.

Spiced Chantilly

⅔ cup + 1⅓ cups whipping cream
½ tsp mixed spices (equal amounts
  of ground cardamom, cinnamon
  and star anise)
1 vanilla bean, split lengthwise
1 cup chopped white chocolate
  (5.3 oz)

Sugar crust

⅓ cup unsalted butter, room
  temperature
½ cup packed brown sugar
¾ cup all-purpose flour
½ tsp kosher salt

Caramelized Apple Éclairs

Serves twelve

Éclairs take a bit of time to prepare, but they're actually not that hard to make. For best results, make each of the components ahead of time, and assemble them at the last minute. The Chantilly cream needs at least eight hours to chill. If you do not have a pastry bag, make one by scooping the choux dough into a resealable plastic bag and cutting a three-quarter-inch hole in one corner. Note that it's difficult to make a smaller batch of éclairs; make the full amount and wrap the leftover, piped éclairs (you'll have at least eight) in plastic wrap and freeze. When you're ready to use them, thaw frozen éclairs on a baking sheet lined with parchment paper before baking them.

Spiced Chantilly Bring ⅔ cup of the cream, the mixed spices and the vanilla bean to a boil in a small pot over high heat. Remove from the heat, cover and allow to infuse for 5 minutes.

Place the chocolate in a large deep, heatproof bowl. Holding a fine-mesh sieve in one hand, carefully pour the infused cream through the sieve directly into the bowl of chocolate. Discard the solids. Using an immersion blender, pulse the mixture to emulsify the ganache. With the blender running, slowly add the 1⅓ cups of cold cream, mixing until well combined. Cover the Chantilly cream with plastic wrap, and refrigerate for at least 8 hours.

Sugar crust Cut 2 large sheets of parchment paper. In a stand mixer fitted with a paddle attachment, beat together all the ingredients until you have a uniform dough.

Set one sheet of parchment paper on a clean work surface, place the dough on top and cover with the second piece. Using a rolling pin, roll the dough into a rectangle of 6 × 12 inches and $^1/_{16}$ inch thick. Slide

Choux pastry

½ cup milk
½ cup water
1 tsp kosher salt
2 tsp white sugar
½ cup unsalted butter, cut into cubes
1 cup all-purpose flour
5 large eggs

Caramelized apple purée

½ cup white sugar
2 Tbsp light corn syrup
4 Cortland apples, cored and cut
  into quarters
1 vanilla bean, split lengthwise
1 Tbsp fresh lemon juice

the dough onto a baking sheet and place in the freezer for 15 minutes, or until the dough is firm.

Using a ruler and a sharp knife, cut the dough into 12 rectangles, each of 5 × 1 inches (reserve any leftovers for another use). Wrap the rectangles of dough well with plastic wrap and freeze until needed.

Choux pastry Preheat the oven to 375°F. Line a baking sheet with parchment paper.

Bring the milk, water, salt, sugar and butter to a boil in a medium pot over high heat. When the butter is melted, remove from the heat and stir in the flour with a rubber spatula or a wooden spoon until the dough comes together. Return the pot to the stove over medium heat and stir for 1 to 2 minutes until the dough pulls away from the side of the pot.

Transfer the dough to a stand mixer fitted with a paddle attachment. Mix at low speed for 1 minute. Add the eggs, one at a time, making sure that each egg is well combined before adding the next one. Mix until the dough is nice and smooth, about 3 minutes.

Spoon the dough into a pastry bag fitted with a plain #9 tip. Pipe 20 éclairs, each 5 inches long, onto the baking sheet, leaving 1 inch around each one. (This recipe calls for 12 éclairs. Wrap and freeze any éclairs that you don't plan to cook right away.) Cover each éclair with a rectangle of sugar crust dough, then lower the oven temperature to 350°F and bake for 30 minutes, or until golden and hollow inside. (They should be pretty dry inside. To test for doneness, slice one open horizontally. If they are not fully cooked, reduce the oven temperature to 300°F and return the éclairs to the oven for 10 minutes or so.) Remove the éclairs from the heat, and allow them come to room temperature before cutting them.

recipe continued overleaf...

Caramelized apple purée Combine the sugar and corn syrup in a medium pot. Add just enough water to cover the sugar and cook over high heat, without stirring, to obtain a medium caramel, about 4 minutes (use a candy thermometer and look for around 360°F). Remove the caramel from the heat, and stir in the apples, the vanilla bean and the lemon juice.

Reduce the heat to medium-low heat and cook the apples in the caramel for 15 minutes, or until they are very soft. Remove from the heat and allow the mixture to cool to room temperature. Remove and discard the vanilla bean.

Transfer the apple mixture to a blender and purée until smooth. Scoop into a bowl, cover with plastic wrap and refrigerate until cool.

To assemble Use a bread knife to cut horizontally through each éclair. Set the top halves aside. Spoon the apple purée into a pastry bag fitted with a small tip, then pipe a line of purée along each éclair.

Scoop the Chantilly cream mixture into the bowl of a stand mixer fitted with a whisk attachment. Beat at medium speed for about 1 minute until the cream forms soft peaks. Spoon the whipped cream into a pastry bag fitted with a medium tip, and pipe the Chantilly cream over the purée. Place the top half of each éclair over the filling. Serve immediately.

Preservation Society

—— chef ——

CAMILLA WYNNE

Camilla Wynne grew up in Alberta eating her grandmothers' preserves, both sweet and savoury, but it wasn't until years later that she took any interest in learning the recipes herself. After beginning a degree in religious studies at McGill, she found herself baking her way through mid-terms and promptly decamped for pastry school at the Institut de tourisme et d'hôtellerie du Québec. It was during her *stage* with Patrice Demers at Les Chèvres that she made her first marmalade from real citrus fruit and got hooked on preserving. And we're glad she did! That *stage* led to a few more years of work with Patrice, then at Anise, Laloux and Pâtisserie Rhubarbe.

While touring with her rock band, she continued to experiment with preserves, and when the band broke up, she began Preservation Society to sell her products to restaurants and teach others how to can and preserve. We like to visit the shop in Mile End to peruse the latest products made from local ingredients and sample her creative spins on popular flavour combinations, such as a unique concoction of celery pickled in a Bloody Caesar–flavoured brine. She offers workshops, writes cookbooks and generally shares her love and knowledge of preserving; her products can be found in many specialty shops in Montreal, but do try to pop by the Ritz-Carlton bar for a drink and one of her accoutrements.

facing STAINED GLASS JAM

2¼ lbs peeled, diced Flemish
   Beauty pears (about 8 whole)
4 cups fresh or frozen cranberries
3¾ cups (26 ½ oz/750 g) white sugar
2 star anise
2 lemons

Makes six ½-pint (1 cup) jars

Stained Glass Jam

The creamy white chunks of pear suspended behind glass in vibrant red cranberry jelly inspired the name of this jam. It pays homage to our beautiful fall fruits as well as to the magnificent churches full of stained glass that awed me when I first moved to Montreal. This jam reminds me of a clean, minimalist mincemeat. You could certainly use it to fill tarts, but it's equally good with scones, on top of a panna cotta or stirred into yogurt.

In a large pot or preserving pan, combine the pears, cranberries, sugar and star anise. Wash and dry the lemons, then remove the peel in long strips using a vegetable peeler. Stack the strips on a cutting board to slice them crosswise into thin strips. Juice the lemons and add to the pear mixture along with the julienned lemon zest. Allow to stand briefly to macerate.

In the meantime, have ready six ½-pint (1 cup) glass jars with sealable lids, and wash them well with soapy water. Place a wire rack or a tea towel in the bottom of a large pot or boiling water canner, fill it with water and bring to a boil over high heat. Using tongs, place the jars into the boiling water and boil for 10 minutes. Remove from the heat and allow the jars to sit in the hot water until ready to use.

Bring the pear mixture to a boil over medium-high heat. Boil hard, stirring often, until the setting point is reached (to test this, dip a teaspoon into the jam, and place it on a cold plate in the freezer for 2 minutes; if it wrinkles like a silk shirt when pushed gently with a finger, it is ready). Remove from the heat and allow to rest for 5 minutes, stirring occasionally. Remove and discard the star anise pods.

Remove the jars from the water and drain, and bring the water back up to a boil. Ladle the jam into the hot sterilized jars, filling them to within ¼ inch of the rim. Run a plastic spatula or a wooden chopstick around the edges of the jars to remove any air bubbles, and wipe the rims. Place the lids on the jars and screw the bands on until they are fingertip-tight.

Process the jars in the boiling water for 10 minutes. Using a jar lifter, transfer the jars to a dish rack or to a tea towel placed on the counter and allow to cool, undisturbed, for 24 hours.

After 24 hours, check the seal (you should be able to remove the screw band and turn the jar upside down without the lid falling off!). If the jar has not sealed properly, refrigerate it and consume the contents over the next few months. Try to wait at least 3 weeks before opening properly sealed jars—you will be rewarded with a far more balanced flavour. Sealed jars will keep in a cool, dark place for up to 1 year.

3 lbs fresh blackberries
2½ tsp grated fresh ginger
6 small shallots, thinly sliced
1¼ cups + 2 Tbsp white sugar
½ tsp salt
½ tsp ground black pepper
¼ tsp ground cloves
1 large beet, peeled and grated
    (¾ cup)
¾ cup cider vinegar
¼ cup balsamic vinegar

Blackberry and Beet Chutney

Makes five ½-pint (1 cup) jars

Technically Quebec is not known for its blackberries—they're more of a West Coast standby. But maybe that's what makes it so special when I get great ones here in Montreal. M. Legault, my berry idol since I first tasted his strawberries in 2003, has a small amount of the most excellent blackberries every year. This summer, once I felt I'd exhausted their sweet possibilities with jams and butters and syrups, I came up with this chutney. A little beet brings an earthiness to ground the sweet-and-sour flavours. It pairs well with game, pork, cheese. For an easy brunch dish or vegetarian main, dot it onto puff pastry tarts with goat cheese and a little fresh thyme.

Have ready five ½-pint (1 cup) glass jars with sealable lids, and wash them well with soapy water. Place a wire rack or a tea towel in the bottom of a large pot or boiling water canner, fill it with water and bring to a boil over high heat. Using tongs, place the jars into the boiling water and boil for 10 minutes. Remove from the heat and allow the jars to sit in the hot water until ready to use.

In a large, heavy-bottomed pot, combine all the ingredients. Bring to a boil over medium-high heat, stirring to dissolve the sugar. Simmer, stirring occasionally and gradually reducing the heat to medium-low, until the mixture thickens to a jammy consistency. This should take about 25 minutes. Remove from the heat.

Remove the jars from the water and drain, and bring the water back up to a boil. Ladle the chutney into the hot jars, filling them to within ½ inch of the rim. Run a plastic spatula or a wooden chopstick around the edges of the jars to remove any air bubbles, and wipe the rims. Place the lids on the jars and screw the bands on until they are fingertip-tight.

Process the jars in the boiling water for 10 minutes. Using a jar lifter, transfer the jars to a dish rack or to a tea towel placed on the counter and allow to cool, undisturbed, for 24 hours.

After 24 hours, check the seal (you should be able to remove the screw band and turn the jar upside down without the lid falling off!). If the jar has not sealed properly, refrigerate it and consume the contents over the next few months. Try to wait at least 3 weeks before opening properly sealed jars—you will be rewarded with a far more balanced flavour. Sealed jars will keep in a cool, dark place for up to 1 year.

Le Quartier Général

—— chef ——

NICOLAS FICUCIELLO

As neighbourhood bistros go, Le Quartier Général in the Plateau is one of the best. The restaurant is flooded with natural light, serves expertly prepared meals by Chef Nicolas Ficuciello and has a "bring your own wine" policy. The service is attentive yet friendly, and the place is so popular, in fact, that reservations are often hard to come by. But persevere: the food is worth the wait.

Nicolas, like many great chefs, developed a passion for cooking at a young age. He grew up surrounded by olive groves, the scent of fresh thyme and rosemary and fresh vegetables pulled from his grandparents' garden. After attending chefs' school at the Ecole Paul Augier in Nice, he broadened his skills in premier restaurants in the South of France and in notable local restaurants such as Renoir at the Sofitel and Graziella downtown. At Le Quartier Général, he continues the tradition of simple but innovative Italian and Niçoise cuisine sourced from fresh market ingredients and farm products. There's no doubt why it was voted one of the best new restaurants by *enRoute* magazine in 2010 and is still going strong today.

facing SUCKLING PIG TARTS WITH PEARS, BRUSSELS SPROUTS, BACON AND LEMONY SOUR CREAM

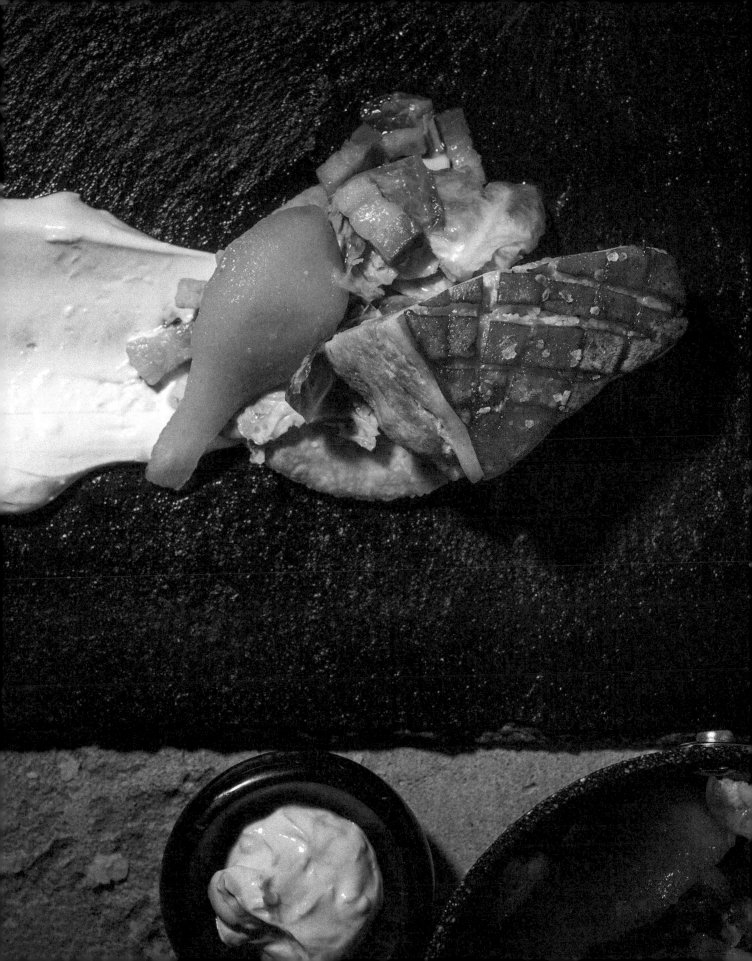

Pie crust

1 cup all-purpose flour
1 tsp kosher salt
½ cup unsalted butter, cold,
    cut into small cubes
1 large egg
2 Tbsp water, cold

Lemony sour cream

1¾ cups sour cream
⅓ cup whipping cream
zest of 1 lemon
salt and pepper

Suckling Pig Tarts with Pears, Brussels Sprouts, Bacon and Lemony Sour Cream

Serves four

Suckling pig is a milk-fed piglet, and this recipe is made with the leg, which includes a piece of the inside round or of the sirloin tip. You can find this meat in fine butcher shops, or use pork instead of piglet. Prepare the topping ingredients while the pie crust is resting.

Pie crust Place the flour and salt in a medium bowl and mix well. Add the butter and, using your fingertips, rub the butter into the flour until the mixture is uniform and resembles coarse bread crumbs. Make a well in the centre.

In a small bowl, lightly beat the egg and water. Pour the mixture into the well, quickly working it into the flour mixture until it is thoroughly blended. Shape the dough into a ball, wrap well in plastic wrap and reserve at room temperature for 1 hour.

Lemony sour cream In a medium bowl, mix the sour cream, whipping cream and zest until well combined. Season with salt and pepper, and refrigerate until serving.

Finish pie crust Preheat the oven to 400°F. Cut 2 large sheets of parchment paper. Have handy a 4-inch round cookie cutter or a glass with a 4-inch mouth.

Using a sharp knife, cut the dough in half. Set one sheet of paper on a clean work surface, place one piece of the dough on top and cover with the second sheet. Using a rolling pin or a bottle, roll the dough $1/16$ inch thick. Cut two 4-inch rounds and place them on a baking sheet. Repeat with the second half. (You should have 4 tart shells.) Bake for 10 minutes, remove from the oven and allow to cool on the baking sheet.

Seared suckling pig

1½ to 2 lbs suckling pig leg (or pork
  eye of round)
4 oz bacon, cut in small dice
4 Bosc pears
2 Tbsp butter
¼ cup white sugar
15 Brussels sprouts, trimmed and
  separated into leaves
salt and pepper
olive oil for drizzling

Seared suckling pig Preheat the oven to 400°F.

Using a sharp knife, score the fatty side of the pig in a cross-hatch pattern about ¼ inch deep. Heat an ovenproof sauté pan over medium heat, add the pig, fatty side down, and sear on both side until golden, 6 to 7 minutes per side.

Place the pan in the oven and cook for 10 minutes, or until the internal temperature reaches 145°F. Remove the pig from the oven, allow it to cool slightly, then cut the meat into 4 portions. Set aside.

Heat a small sauté pan over low heat and add the bacon. Cook until the meat is cooked and the fat has rendered, about 5 minutes. Drain off any excess fat and set aside.

Peel and core the pears, then cut them lengthwise into 8 wedges. Discard the peel and core. Melt the butter in a small sauté pan over low heat and add the sugar. Stir in the pears and cook for 2 minutes on each side. Add the cooked bacon and the Brussels sprouts leaves. Season with salt and pepper and continue to cook for 30 seconds.

To assemble Smear a tablespoonful of the lemon sour cream in the centre of a small serving plate. Set a tart shell on top. Spoon a small dollop of the sour cream on the pastry, then cover with one-quarter of the pear–Brussels sprouts mixture. Top with a piece of the pig meat and drizzle with olive oil.

Beef short ribs
1 beef short rib with bone
  (English-cut), about 3 lbs
1 onion, peeled and cut in small dice
1 carrot, peeled and cut in small dice
2 celery stalks, peeled and cut in
  small dice
4 cups red wine
4 cups water
1 bay leaf

Celeriac purée
¼ cup butter
1 onion, cut in small dice
2 cups whipping cream
4 celeriacs, peeled and cut
  in small dice
salt and pepper

Salsa verde
2 bunches fresh parsley, washed,
  patted dry and chopped
¼ cup capers, rinsed, drained and
  crushed
¼ cup finely chopped pickles
¾ cup olive oil
 salt and pepper

Braised Beef Short Ribs, Salsa Verde and Celeriac Purée

Serves four

Beef short ribs Preheat the oven to 325°F. Trim the fat, cut the silverskin from the short rib and discard.

Heat a sauté pan over high heat, add the meat and cook until browned on all sides, about 5 minutes. Transfer the meat to a roasting pan.

Return the sauté pan to the heat, add the onions, carrots and celery and cook until slightly browned, about 5 minutes. Deglaze the pan with the wine and water, bring to a boil and pour over the meat. Add the bay leaf. Cover with aluminum foil and cook for about 4 hours, until the meat is tender and falls from the bone.

Celeriac purée Melt the butter in a medium saucepan over medium-low heat. Add the onions and the cream and cook gently until the onions are soft and confit, 20 to 30 minutes. Stir in the celeriac, cover and cook, stirring occasionally, until tender, 30 minutes.

Transfer the mixture to a blender and purée until smooth. Set a fine-mesh sieve over a clean bowl. Press the purée through the strainer and discard the solids. Season with salt and pepper to taste. Set aside.

Salsa verde Combine the parsley, capers and pickles in a small bowl. Add the olive oil and toss until well coated. Season with salt and pepper. Will keep refrigerated in an airtight container for up to 3 days.

To serve Spoon one-quarter of the celeriac purée into the bottom of each shallow bowl. Divide the short ribs evenly among the bowls, drizzle with the pan juices and garnish with salsa verde.

RUSTIQUE

BREUVAGES CHAUDS

epic espresso	2.39$
allongé	2.39$
americano	2.61$
macchiato	2.61$
cappuccino	3.26$
latté	3.48$
latté en bol	4.34$
mocha	3.91$
chocolat chaud	3.91$
thé	2.61$
breuvages saisonniers	3.91$

quinzaine les saveurs +0.43$

- LATTÉ CHAI
- LATTÉ AU CARAMEL
- LATTÉ À LA VANILLE
- LONDON FOG

TARTELETTES
1.95$ ch.
6/12$ · 12/20$

TAR
19-24

GÂTEAUX
45-50

BARRES, TRANCHES, BISCUITS ET +
1.50-3.91

Rustique

—— *chef* ——

TAMERA CLARK

If you have memories of buying home-made pies from a farm stand on a rural back road or making your own with fruit from the backyard, Rustique in St-Henri is worth a visit. Chef Tamera Clark grew up in a family of home cooks in Vancouver, attended the Pacific Institute of Culinary Arts and then travelled to the Cayman Islands to work as a pastry chef. But she was lured north again in 2013 by her two partners, Ryan Bloom whose cottage gatherings always featured a fruit pie from the stand down the road and Jacqueline Berman who is so devoted to desserts that she's known to sneak one in *before* meals.

Rustique is as quaint as a pie stand and as well stocked with handcrafted desserts, from pies and scones to cookies and old-fashioned Hello Dolly bars. The repurposed wood flooring and oak ceiling recall old farmhouses redolent of warm butter, cinnamon and cooked fruits. The white walls, glass dessert case, chalkboard menu and industrial-whisk lighting keep the room bright and modern. We are huge fans of the apple pie, and we can never pass up a lemon bar or a mini-pie on the way out. Although why go mini if you can go big with this Rustique pear pie recipe?

Pie crust

2 cups pastry flour
1 tsp kosher salt
1 Tbsp white sugar
⅔ cup unsalted butter, cold,
   cut into walnut-sized cubes
⅓ cup cold water
1 large egg yolk
¼ cup whipping cream
 pinch of salt
¼ cup raw sugar

Pear filling

4 large pears
2 Tbsp fresh lemon juice
⅓ cup butter
⅓ cup white sugar
2 Tbsp cornstarch
¼ tsp salt
 2 tsp ground cinnamon
¾ tsp ground ginger
½ tsp ground nutmeg
⅓ cup cold water
½ tsp almond extract

*Serves 8
(makes one
10-inch pie)*

Rustique Pear Galette

Prepare the pie dough ahead of time so the pastry has time to chill before baking. This step allows the dough to relax, which makes it less elastic, easier to roll out and less likely to shrink while baking (less crust is never a good thing!).

This recipe can be made with a variety of seasonal fruits, such as apples, plums, peaches and pears or a combination of two or more flavours. Be creative—that's what the kitchen is for. I often pair pear and almonds, and I mostly go with the Bartlett variety that provides lots of juice when fully ripe. And I love my pie served with ice cream, but then again I think everything is better with ice cream. *Bon appétit!*

Pie crust

Combine the flour, salt and white sugar in a medium bowl. Add the butter, and use your fingers to toss the cubes through the flour mixture. Add the water a little at a time and use your fingers to work the butter, flour mixture and water together to form a dough. (Try not to break down the butter. Larger chunks mean a flakier crust.) The dough should not be wet or sticky; if it is too dry, add more water, 1 Tbsp at a time, until the dough comes together. Do not overmix dough either, or it will become tough and you will lose the flaky texture.

Press the dough into a flat disc, wrap it in plastic wrap and refrigerate for at least 3 hours or up to 2 days. Allow the dough to stand at room temperature for 10 minutes before you use it. This will allow for easier rolling of the dough.

Pear filling Peel and core the pears, and cut them into eighths. Place the pear slices in a medium bowl, add the lemon juice and toss well to coat.

Melt the butter in a large sauté pan over high heat. Add the pears and cook until slightly brown, 5 to 7 minutes. Reduce the heat to medium-high and cook until the fruit is softened, 10 to 12 minutes more.

In a small bowl, combine the sugar, cornstarch, salt, cinnamon, ginger and nutmeg until well mixed. Stir the ⅓ cup water, almond extract and the dry ingredients into the pears and cook until thick, about 1 minute. Remove from the heat and allow the filling to cool completely, about 30 minutes, before using. (If the filling is too warm when you assemble your pie, it will melt the butter in your pastry dough. This will make it very hard to form a beautiful galette crust.)

Finish pie crust Have ready a 14-inch plate and a 10-inch pie pan. In a small bowl, whisk together the egg yolk, cream and a pinch of salt. This is your egg wash.

Lightly dust a work surface with flour. Using a rolling pin, roll out the dough until it is ⅛ inch thick. Place the plate on the dough, then cut around it with a sharp knife. Roll the dough onto the rolling pin and carefully lift the crust into the pie pan. Centre the dough and allow the excess to fall evenly over the edges of the dish.

Spoon the cooled pear filling into the pie crust. Starting at one point along the crust, fold the excess dough over the filling, then gradually turn the pie, folding the crust as you go, so all the excess crust covers the filling (you will have a galette— the centre will be free of pie crust). Using a pastry brush, brush the crust with the egg wash and sprinkle it with the raw sugar. Place the pie in the freezer for about 15 minutes to firm the dough.

Preheat the oven to 425°F. Remove the chilled pie from the freezer and bake it for 15 minutes. Reduce the oven temperature to 375°F and continue to bake until the crust is golden and the filling is bubbling, about 1 hour. Allow the pie to cool slightly before digging in, as the fruit can be very hot straight from the oven.

Shortbread base
½ lb cold butter, diced
½ cup white sugar
2 cups all-purpose flour
⅛ tsp salt

Lemon filling
2¼ cups white sugar
¾ cup all-purpose flour
1½ Tbsp lemon zest
5 large eggs
¾ cup fresh lemon juice
icing sugar for dusting

Makes
12 bars

Lemon Bars

Shortbread base Preheat the oven to 350°F. Line a 13 × 18-inch baking sheet that has a 1-inch rim with parchment paper.

Combine all the ingredients in a food processor and pulse until the mixture has a sand-like consistency. Lightly press the shortbread dough evenly into the pan, and bake for 15 to 20 minutes, or until very light brown. Transfer the baking sheet to a wire rack and allow to cool while you prepare the filling.

Lemon filling Reduce the oven temperature to 325°F. In a large bowl, whisk together the sugar, flour and lemon zest. Set aside.

In a second bowl, whisk together the eggs and lemon juice. When you are ready to bake the bars, gradually whisk the dry ingredients into the egg mixture until

smooth (the filling will become gummy if it sits for too long). Pour the lemon filling over the cooled shortbread crust and bake for 25 to 30 minutes, until the filling is set. (It should be firm yet still soft to the touch.) Remove from the oven and allow the bars to cool to room temperature.

Cut the bars into whatever size you prefer—large, small, there's no judgement here! Will keep refrigerated in an airtight container for up to 1 week. When ready to serve, dust with icing sugar to impress your guests (or yourself!). Good job. Enjoy!

Le St-Urbain

— *chef* —

MARC-ANDRÉ ROYAL

Marc-André Royal was born in Montreal, but he spent his formative years apprenticing near Whistler, British Columbia, where he was able to nurture his passion for snowboarding as well as cooking. After stints at Araxi and Blue Water, as well as L'Express in Montreal, he worked in London at Club Gascon, a one-star Michelin restaurant. In 2008, he returned home to open Le St-Urbain, a modern neighbourhood bistro in Ahuntsic with a seasonally focused menu.

We love that his dishes, including an exquisite smoked goose liver, are accompanied by three or four vegetables sourced from local farms but also from Le St-Urbain's own garden in Blainville and highlighted on the restaurant's blackboard menu. We also love the wine menu, which is one of North America's most extensive, and always complements the food. And since Marc-André opened his own bakery, La Bête à Pain, just a few steps away from the restaurant in 2011, we always look forward to the freshly baked bread—which was the last thing on Le St-Urbain's menu that Marc-André hadn't made himself.

Ganache

2¼ cups dark chocolate
   (70% cocoa), roughly chopped
4 gelatin sheets
2 cups milk
¾ cup whipping cream

Buttermilk ice cream

12 large egg yolks
⅓ cup white sugar
3 vanilla beans, seeds scraped
   and pods discarded
2 cups buttermilk
¾ cup whipping cream

Chocolate "Crémeux" with Buttermilk Ice Cream

*Serves
six*

Ganache Have ready six 2-oz ramekins. Set the chocolate in a large heatproof bowl.

Place the gelatin in a small bowl, cover with ice water and allow to bloom for about 10 minutes.

Place the milk and cream in a medium saucepan. Drain the gelatin and add it to the milk and cream, and bring to a simmer over medium heat. Pour the hot liquid over the chocolate and stir well until emulsified. Pour into individual ramekins and refrigerate for at least 2 hours.

Buttermilk ice cream In the bowl of a stand mixer fitted with a paddle attachment, cream the egg yolks and sugar at high speed for 3 minutes. Beat in the vanilla seeds, buttermilk and cream until well combined.

Pour the ice cream base into a medium saucepan and warm over medium-low heat, stirring continuously, until the mixture is 175°F. (Test the temperature with an instant-read thermometer.) Pour the mixture into a stainless steel bowl, cover with plastic wrap and refrigerate for 24 hours.

Pour the mixture into an ice cream maker and process according to the manufacturer's instructions.

To serve Simply garnish each chocolate "crémeux" with a quenelle of ice cream.

Minus 8 caramel

¼ cup white sugar

2 Tbsp smashed lemon grass

¼ cup Minus 8 vinegar (or aged
   sherry vinegar)

Pickled mustard seeds

½ cup yellow mustard seeds

1 cup seasoned rice vinegar

1 cup water

½ cup white sugar

Pickled carrot pearls

1 large carrot, peeled

1 cup seasoned rice vinegar

¼ cup vegetable stock

Boudin Fermier with Celeriac Purée, Miso-Braised Carrots, Minus 8 Caramel and Pickled Mustard Seeds

*Serves
6 to 8*

Boudin is a classic French-style blood sausage. It uses fresh pig's blood and the fat from a pig's back, both of which can be bought at a good butcher shop. It's not hard to make boudin, but it can be a little messy. The result, though, is delicious. It has a perfect balance of onion, spices and seasonings. Minus 8 vinegar is a unique wine vinegar from Ontario that uses grapes picked at –8°C (18°F) and crushed while still frozen. The juice is then fermented and aged in French oak barrels, which results in a raisin-like darkness and gentle sweetness. Seasoned rice vinegar can be found at any Japanese grocery store. Serve this dish with a nice salad of fresh herbs: chervil, chives, tarragon and parsley.

Minus 8 caramel Place the sugar in a small, heavy-bottomed sauté pan and set it over high heat, without stirring, for 2 to 3 minutes to dissolve the sugar. If the sugar is browning too fast around the edges, tilt the pan around to move the sugar. Once the sugar turns dark amber, remove from the heat and immediately add the lemon grass and vinegar. Stir to combine. Allow to rest for 1 hour to infuse.

Strain the vinegar mixture through a fine sieve, discard the solids and set aside.

Pickled mustard seeds Place the mustard seeds, vinegar, water and sugar into a small saucepan over medium-high heat. Bring to a boil and then reduce the heat to low, simmering until the seeds are tender and the liquid has reduced to about one-third the original volume and resembles a thick syrup. Refrigerate until cool.

Pickled carrot pearls Using a Parisian spoon or a small melon baller that is about the size of a pearl, make small "pearls" of carrot. Combine the vinegar and stock in a small pot, and bring to a boil over high heat. Add the carrot pearls and remove the

Blood pudding

6 cups diced pork fat
6 cups diced onions
2 tsp ground star anise
2 tsp ground cloves
2 tsp ground cinnamon
2 tsp ground allspice
2 tsp ground ginger
5 Tbsp kosher salt
12 cups pig's blood, room
    temperature

Medjool date purée

10 Medjool dates, pitted
1 cup fresh orange juice
1 cup vegetable stock
1 cinnamon stick
1 star anise

Miso-braised carrots

6 large carrots
4 cups vegetable stock
3 Tbsp red miso paste
3 Tbsp honey
2 Tbsp unsalted butter

ingredients continued…

pot from the heat. Allow to cool for about 10 minutes. Remove the pearls from the pot and set aside.

Chill the pickling liquid in the fridge; when it's cold, add the carrot pearls. Keep refrigerated until ready to serve.

Blood pudding Preheat the oven to 275°F. Have ready an 8-inch square pan.

Melt the pork fat in a medium saucepan over medium heat. Add the onions, star anise, cloves, cinnamon, allspice, ginger and salt and cook, stirring occasionally, for 8 to 10 minutes.

Scrape the onion mixture into the pan. Pour the pig's blood overtop and mix until well combined. Bake for 1 hour. Keep warm.

Medjool date purée Combine all of the ingredients in a small saucepan and bring to a boil over medium-high heat. Reduce the heat to medium, and simmer until the dates are very soft and falling apart and the cooking liquid is one-quarter of the original volume. Remove the cinnamon

stick and anise from the saucepan and discard.

Place the mixture in a blender and blend until smooth. Add a touch of vegetable stock if the mixture isn't coming together. Strain the mixture through a fine-mesh sieve and keep warm.

Miso-braised carrots Cut the carrots into 1½-inch rounds, keeping them as equal as possible to ensure even cooking.

Place the stock, miso and honey into a medium saucepan and bring to a simmer over medium-high heat, whisking to dissolve the honey and miso. Add the carrots, bring back to a simmer and cook until carrots are just tender, 8 to 10 minutes. Remove the carrots from the cooking liquid using a slotted spoon, and set aside.

Place the saucepan with the liquid back on medium-high heat, and reduce the cooking liquid until it's one-quarter the original volume and starts to thicken and become a glaze, about 20 minutes.

recipe continued overleaf…

Celeriac purée
1 large celeriac, peeled
¼ cup + 1 Tbsp unsalted butter
1 medium Vidalia onion, sliced
8 garlic cloves, peeled and smashed
3 cups vegetable stock
1 cup whipping cream
kosher salt to taste

Charred Brussels sprouts
1 Tbsp canola oil
12 Brussels sprouts
3 Tbsp water
salt to taste

Garnishes
2 small multi-coloured carrots
fennel fronds

Celeriac purée Cut the celeriac into 1 × 1-inch pieces so that they cook evenly. Melt the ¼ cup butter in a medium pot over medium-low heat. Add the celeriac, onions and garlic. Stir just to coat with the butter, cover and reduce the heat to low. Cook the vegetables for 25 minutes, or until the onions are translucent and quite soft, stirring every 5 to 7 minutes.

Add the stock and cream and bring to a rolling simmer over medium-high heat. Cook, uncovered, until the liquid has reduced to about one-third the original volume and the celeriac is almost falling apart. Place the hot vegetables and half of the cooking liquid in a blender and process; it's important that the mixture is hot so that it blends easily. If the purée has trouble coming together, add more of the cooking liquid in small increments.

Finish by blending in the 1 Tbsp butter and salt to taste. Strain the mixture through a fine-mesh sieve to make a very smooth purée. Keep warm.

Charred Brussels sprouts Heat a medium sauté pan over high heat and add the canola oil. When the pan is hot, add the Brussels sprouts, cut side down. Cook until dark and caramelized, about 4 minutes. Add the 3 Tbsp water, cover the pan and allow to steam for 2 minutes. Season with salt and set aside.

To finish Have ready a bowl of ice water. Using a vegetable peeler, peel thin shavings of the carrots into the bowl of water. Allow to chill for 5 minutes.

Finish the miso-braised carrots by reheating the cooking glaze over medium-high heat. Add the reserved carrots and butter. Toss together to warm the carrots and cover them with glaze. Slice the blood pudding.

Add a spoonful of the celeriac purée to the centre of a serving plate. Place a square of the blood pudding on top. Take a couple of spoonfuls of the date purée and drizzle it around. Scatter the miso carrots, pickled carrots and charred Brussels sprouts around the blood pudding. Place a small spoonful of the pickled mustard seeds on top. Drizzle the Minus 8 caramel over the pudding to finish. Garnish with fennel fronds and the shaved carrots.

Sel Gras

—— chef ——
MARCO SANTOS

Just days after opening in 2013, Sel Gras was firebombed and burned to the ground. With the support of the neighbourhood, friends and family, the restaurant has risen from the ashes and found an eager following in Mile End. Chef Marco Santos has created a varied menu that draws on the Mediterranean with nods to Asia and South America. The ingredients, however, are local and seasonal, including braised game meats and confit root vegetables in the winter, grilled fish and fresh berries in the summer. True to the restaurant's name, natural seasonings—often *sel* (salt) and *gras* (fat)—are indispensable to this chef's kitchen.

The restaurant has gained a great reputation for its decadent brunches, which bring together an eclectic crowd from nearby Mile End, but it's their evening menu that speaks to us with Chef Marco's selection of game meat dishes. The elk tataki with cucumber rémoulade, sultanas and toasted coconut with red wine syrup not only looks tantalizing but is also a pleasure to eat, especially if you can master this dish at home. The miso-marinated black cod is a Montreal favourite as well.

facing ELK TATAKI WITH RED WINE SYRUP, CUCUMBER RÉMOULADE AND TOASTED COCONUT

Roasted garlic oil

2 cups canola oil
2 garlic bulbs, cloves separated
   and cut in half

Red wine syrup

2 cups red wine
¾ cup white sugar
1 cinnamon stick
1 bay leaf
1 sprig fresh thyme

Cucumber rémoulade

4 cups grated celeriac (1 large
   celeriac)
2 shallots, thinly chopped
½ English cucumber, unpeeled
   and finely diced
⅓ cup mayonnaise
⅓ cup sour cream
2 tsp grainy mustard
2 Tbsp fresh lemon juice
zest of 1 lemon
salt and pepper to taste

Spice-rubbed elk tataki

4 tsp coriander seeds
4 tsp fennel seeds
4 tsp Montreal steak spice
2 elk filets mignon, each 7 oz
salt
olive oil
2 Tbsp sultana raisins for garnish

Elk Tataki with Red Wine Syrup, Cucumber Rémoulade and Toasted Coconut

Serves 4 to 6

Have ready four to six 3 to 4-inch ring moulds. It's worth seeking out elk meat from a local elk farmer or a specialty butcher shop, but you can also use venison or beef sirloin in this recipe. And you should be able to find Montreal steak spice in the spice aisle of most grocery stores. To save time, you can brown the croutons and toast the coconut at the same time in a 375°F oven, but watch them carefully because the coconut cooks faster than the croutons. You'll need about three minutes for the coconut and double that for the croutons.

Roasted garlic oil Bring the canola oil to a boil in a medium saucepan over high heat. Reduce the heat to low, add the garlic and simmer for 40 minutes.

Place a fine-mesh sieve over a large heatproof bowl, then strain the oil into it. Discard the garlic and set aside.

Red wine syrup Pour the red wine into a medium saucepan, then add the sugar, cinnamon, bay leaf and thyme. Bring to a boil over high heat and then reduce the heat so that the red wine is just boiling. Cook for 10 to 15 minutes, or until the mixture thickens enough to lightly coat the back of a spoon.

Place a fine-mesh sieve over a medium heatproof bowl, then strain the syrup into it. Discard the solids. Refrigerate the syrup, uncovered, until cool.

Cucumber rémoulade Combine all of the ingredients in a large bowl and blend until well mixed.

Spice-rubbed elk tataki Preheat the oven to 350°F. Place the coriander and fennel seeds in an ovenproof frying pan or metal pie plate and roast for 4 minutes, until slightly browned and fragrant. (You can

Croutons
1 day-old white baguette, cut into
    small cubes
olive oil for drizzling

Toasted coconut
2 Tbsp unsweetened shredded
    coconut

also roast the spices on the stovetop in a small, dry frying pan over high heat for 3 to 4 minutes.) Remove from the oven, transfer to a cold plate and allow to cool to room temperature.

Place the coriander and fennel seeds in a spice mill or a coffee grinder. Add the steak spice and process until you have a fine powder. (If you don't have a grinder, use a mortar and pestle.) This is your rub mixture.

Set the elk meat on a baking sheet and season with salt. Sprinkle completely with the rub mixture. Heat olive oil in a large frying pan over high heat. Add the meat and sear for 30 to 45 seconds per side. Remove from the heat and allow to cool. Using a very sharp knife, slice the meat into very thin slices.

Croutons Preheat the oven to 375°F. Arrange the bread in a single layer on a baking sheet and drizzle with olive oil. Toss well to coat. Bake for 6 minutes, lightly toss the croutons and cook for another 2 minutes or until golden, 6 to 8 minutes total.

Toasted coconut Preheat the oven to 375°F. Arrange the coconut in a single layer on a small baking sheet and cook for 3 to 5 minutes, or until golden.

To assemble Place a ring mould in the centre of each plate. Fill the mould with rémoulade to a depth of three-quarters. Gently remove the mould. Top each serving of rémoulade with 4 to 5 slices of elk tataki. Drizzle with red wine syrup, then garnish with a small handful of croutons. Drizzle garlic oil around the plate and in a circle over the meat. Sprinkle coconut and sultanas over the plate.

Marinated black cod

4 to 6 skinless black cod (sablefish) fillets, each 7 oz
2 cups tamari
½ cup red miso paste
1 cup cold water
scant ½ cup honey
2 Tbsp sambal oelek
1-inch piece of fresh ginger, chopped
3 garlic cloves, peeled and halved

Mushroom broth

3 Tbsp olive oil
3 cups fresh shiitake mushrooms, caps removed and set aside, but stems reserved
1 carrot, cut in 1-inch dice
1 onion, cut in 1-inch dice

2 large celery stalks, cut in 1-inch dice
2 to 3 garlic cloves, peeled
1 Tbsp thinly sliced fresh unpeeled ginger
3 bay leaves (or 4 small ones)
2 Tbsp tamari
4 cups water
salt to taste

Miso- and Tamari-Marinated Black Cod with Parsnip Purée, Sautéed Shiitakes, Deep-Fried Brussels Sprouts and "Braz"-Style Potatoes

Serves 4 to 6

Start this dish the day before you plan to serve it so the fish has time to marinate.

Marinated black cod Line a baking sheet with parchment paper, and place the black cod on top.

In a small bowl, combine the tamari, miso, water, honey and sambal oelek until well mixed. Stir in the ginger and garlic and pour over the fish. Refrigerate, covered with plastic wrap, for 12 to 16 hours to allow the fish to marinate.

Mushroom broth Heat 3 Tbsp of the olive oil in a medium saucepan over high heat for 30 seconds. Reduce the heat to medium-low, add the mushroom stems, carrots, onions, celery and garlic and sauté for 5 minutes to bring out the flavours. Stir in the ginger, bay leaves, tamari and water and bring to a boil. Reduce the heat to low and simmer for about 45 minutes. Season to taste with salt.

Place a fine-mesh sieve over a clean saucepan. Strain the broth and discard the solids. Set aside to keep warm.

"Braz"-style potatoes Heat 3 Tbsp of the olive oil in a cast-iron or nonstick frying pan over medium heat. Add the onions, reduce the heat to medium-low and cook, stirring occasionally, until caramelized, about 30 minutes. Set aside.

Preheat a deep fryer to 350°F, or fill a medium, deep-sided pot with canola oil and heat over medium-high heat until it reaches 350°F (use a deep-fry thermometer to test the temperature). Line a large plate with paper towels. Working in batches and keeping your face away from the pot, very carefully drop the matchstick potatoes into the hot oil and cook until golden, 30 to 45 seconds. Using a slotted spoon, transfer the potatoes to the paper towel–lined plate. Set aside.

"Braz"-style potatoes

4 Tbsp olive oil
1 medium to large Spanish onion
    or Vidalia onion, thinly sliced
canola oil for deep-frying
4 to 5 Yukon Gold potatoes (½ potato
    per person + 2 more), cut into
    matchsticks on a mandolin
½ bunch fresh parsley
½ bunch green onions
½ bunch fresh cilantro
⅓ cup + 1 Tbsp canola or grape-
    seed oil
2 to 3 large eggs (½ per person)
sundried cherry tomatoes to taste,
    thinly sliced on a mandolin

Parsnip purée

1 lb parsnips, peeled and cut
    in 1-inch dice (about 4 medium)
1 medium Yukon Gold potato,
    cut in 1-inch dice
1 cup whole milk
salted butter to taste

Sautéed shiitakes and Brussels sprouts

8 to 10 Brussels sprouts,
    cleaned and trimmed
7 Tbsp olive oil
reserved shiitake mushrooms
    (3 cups), sliced
fresh thyme
salt and pepper

Place the parsley, green onions and cilantro in a blender, add ⅓ cup + 1 Tbsp canola (or grapeseed) oil and purée until smooth. Set aside.

Parsnip purée Place the parsnips in a medium saucepan and add the potatoes, milk and, if needed, enough cold water to cover the vegetables. Bring to a boil over high heat, then reduce the heat to medium and simmer until the vegetables are soft, about 30 minutes. Drain well, reserving a bit of the cooking liquid. Transfer the vegetables and the parsnip cooking liquid to a blender, add the butter and purée until very smooth. Set aside to keep warm.

Finish black cod Preheat the oven to 400°F and line a baking sheet with parchment paper.

Remove the fish from the marinade, set it on the baking sheet and cook for 10 to 12 minutes, or until the fish is firm to the touch but flakes easily when poked with a fork. (The trick we use to see if the fish is cooked is watching for the minute the bones come out easily.) Set aside.

Sautéed shiitakes and Brussels sprouts Fill a bowl with ice water. Bring a small pot of salted water to a boil over high heat. Add the Brussels sprouts and cook for 3 to 4 minutes. Using a slotted spoon, transfer the Brussels sprouts to the ice water to stop the cooking. When the Brussels sprouts are cold, cut them in half.

Heat 3 Tbsp of the olive oil in a small saucepan on high heat. Add the Brussels sprouts and sauté, stirring occasionally, until golden and crispy, 2 to 3 minutes. Using a slotted spoon, transfer the Brussels sprouts to a plate.

recipe continued overleaf...

Preheat a sauté pan over high heat. Add 4 Tbsp of olive oil, allow it to reach the smoking point and then add the mushrooms and cook for 2 minutes, stirring infrequently. When the mushrooms are slightly caramelized, add the thyme and salt and pepper and sauté for 1 more minute.

Finish potatoes Whisk the eggs in a small bowl. Return the pan of caramelized onions to medium heat and add the remaining 1 Tbsp olive oil. Stir in the matchstick potatoes, cherry tomatoes and herb purée, mixing well and allowing them to heat through. Add the eggs, stirring until all the ingredients bind together.

To serve Smooth a dollop of parsnip purée into the bottom of each large bowl. Top with a piece of black cod and arrange some shiitakes and Brussels sprouts around the fish. Garnish the fish with some Braz-style potatoes and spoon a bit of the broth around the parsnip purée. Drizzle with olive oil. *Bon appétit!*

La Société

—— *chef* ——

JEAN-PHILIPPE (JP) MIRON

Jean-Philippe (JP) Miron has a deep-rooted passion for discovering his own culinary style and technique. After completing his degree at the Institut de tourisme et d'hôtellerie du Québec, he interned at Scarpetta and Momofuku in New York before returning home to work at Simpléchic and Au Pied de Cochon. Now the executive chef at La Société in the heart of downtown Montreal at the Loews Hotel Vogue, JP and his dedicated crew serve breakfast, lunch and dinner.

The sister restaurant to La Société in Toronto, it is the perfect place for bistro fare. After shopping along Saint Catherine Street, we like to take a break here with a classic French cocktail in one hand and a house-made brioche topped with foie gras terrine in the other. The French onion soup topped with Gruyère gratiné or the silky salmon and beef tartares served with fresh salad and crispy house fries are other favourites. When you need a little French comfort food at home, try JP's pot pie, a variation of a classic 1940s French tourte; or the rich and flavourful cavatelli with braised beef and ricotta. These are recipes that will have your guests inviting themselves over for more.

facing GUINEA HEN AND SWEETBREADS POT PIE

Brine

- 9 cups water
- ¾ cup packed brown sugar
- ⅔ cup coarse salt
- 1 sprig fresh thyme
- 5 bay leaves
- 10 peppercorns
- 1¾ lbs whole guinea hen

Braised thighs

- 3 Tbsp canola oil
- 2 brined guinea hen thighs (method below)
- 2 shallots, chopped
- 1 sprig fresh thyme
- 1¼ cups white wine
- 4 cups guinea hen stock (or chicken stock)

Guinea Hen and Sweetbreads Pot Pie

Serves 2 to 4

Guinea hen is probably my favourite poultry! It's carried by almost every butcher shop in town, but if you have a hard time finding it, you can easily substitute any grain-fed organic chicken. I use an eight-inch cast-iron pan to make my pot pies, but any other ovenproof dish will do.

Brine Place the water, brown sugar and salt in a large, deep saucepan and bring to a boil over high heat. Stir in the thyme, bay leaves and peppercorns, then remove from the heat and refrigerate until cool, about 1 hour.

Place the guinea hen in the cold brine, making sure it is fully submerged, and refrigerate for 2 hours.

Remove the guinea hen, discard the brine and separate the bird into breasts and legs. Reserve the legs (thighs), then remove and discard the bones from the breasts, keeping them whole. Cover the meat and refrigerate.

Braised thighs Preheat the oven to 450°F. Set a fine-mesh sieve over a clean bowl.

Heat the canola oil in an ovenproof frying pan over high heat. Place the thighs, skin side down, in the frying pan and sear for 3 minutes, or until golden. Turn the thighs over, add the shallots and thyme and cook for 2 minutes. Deglaze the pan with white wine and cook until reduced by half, about 5 minutes. Pour in the stock, bring to a boil, cover and then transfer to the oven for 1 hour.

Remove the guinea hen thighs from their cooking liquid. When cool enough to handle, remove and discard the bones. Set the meat aside. Strain the braising liquid through the sieve into the bowl and set aside.

Velouté sauce

½ cup + 2 Tbsp butter
½ cup all-purpose flour
4 cups reserved braising liquid
  (from the thighs)
1 cup button mushrooms
1 cup pearl onions, peeled
1 cup diced carrots
1 cup fresh green peas
1 cup diced uncooked sweetbreads
reserved braised guinea hen thighs
salt

Pot pie

2 Tbsp canola oil
3 Tbsp butter
2 brined guinea hen breasts
  (recipe here)
1 sheet puff pastry, big enough
  to cover your pot
1 large egg, beaten
2 Tbsp water
Maldon salt for sprinkling

Velouté sauce In a medium saucepan, melt 2 Tbsp of the butter over low heat. Slowly whisk in the flour to make a roux, cooking the mixture for 5 minutes. Slowly whisk in the braising liquid until smooth, and cook for 30 minutes, until the sauce thickens.

In another medium saucepan, heat the ½ cup of butter over medium heat. Add the mushrooms, pearl onions and carrots and sauté quickly. Add the sautéed vegetables and the peas to the sauce. Stir in the sweetbreads and the guinea hen meat and season with salt. Remove from the heat and allow to cool to room temperature.

Pot pie Preheat the oven to 450°F. Have ready an 10-inch ovenproof cast-iron frying pan.

Heat the canola oil and butter in the frying pan over high heat. Add the guinea hen breasts and sear for 8 minutes or until lightly browned, then transfer to the oven for 10 minutes to finish the cooking. Remove from the oven, allow the meat to cool slightly and cut into 6 pieces. Transfer the meat to a plate. Reserve the pan and leave the oven on.

Spoon the velouté sauce into the bottom of your ovenproof frying pan and place it in the oven for 3 to 4 minutes to heat up. Arrange the guinea hen pieces evenly on top, then cover the top of the dish with a piece of puff pastry.

In a small bowl, mix the egg and water to make an egg wash. Using a pastry brush or a spoon, cover the puff pastry with a layer of egg wash, then sprinkle with Maldon salt. Bake for 14 minutes or until the puff pastry rises and becomes golden. Serve immediately.

Ricotta
4 cups whole milk
½ cup whipping cream
3 Tbsp fresh lemon juice
salt

Tomato sauce
2 Tbsp olive oil
1 large onion, chopped
1 garlic clove, chopped
salt and pepper
2 cups red wine
2 cans (each 28 oz) crushed San
　Marzano tomatoes (6 cups)
1 lb beef chuck, whole
lots of grated Parmesan

Cavatelli with
Serves four # Braised Beef and Ricotta

Making your own ricotta from scratch is worth the effort in this dish. Have a large piece of cheesecloth on hand, and start the ricotta a day ahead so it has time to drain. In the restaurant, we use a cavatelli maker to shape the pasta. If you do not have one, you can always use a ridged wooden cavatelli paddle (also used to make gnocchi) or the back of a fork to roll them.

Ricotta Place a strainer over a medium bowl and line it with the sheet of cheese-cloth. Set aside.

Heat the milk and cream in a medium saucepan over medium heat until it reaches 180°F (use an instant-read ther-mometer to check the temperature). Whisk in the lemon juice until the mixture starts to curdle, then strain it through the cheesecloth and refrigerate for at least 4 hours but preferably overnight. Season with salt.

Tomato sauce Heat the olive oil in a large saucepan on medium heat. Add the onions and garlic and season with salt and pepper. Stir in the red wine and cook until reduced by half, about 10 minutes. Add the tomatoes and bring to a simmer.

While the tomato sauce is simmering, season the beef with salt. Heat a large frying pan on high heat, add the beef, sear on all sides until golden and then add it to the sauce. Reduce the heat to low and simmer for 3 hours or until the beef is cooked and easy to shred.

Cavatelli
7 cups tipo "00" flour
1 lb fresh ricotta (recipe here)
+ more for garnish
pinch of salt
3 Tbsp water

Cavatelli In a stand mixer fitted with a paddle attachment, combine the flour with the ricotta and salt at low speed until well mixed. With the motor running, slowly add the water until the dough is smooth. Gather the dough into a ball, wrap it in plastic wrap and refrigerate for 30 minutes.

Lightly dust a clean work surface with flour. Unwrap the dough and cut it into 10 equal pieces. Using your hands, roll each piece into a log ¼ inch in diameter. Lightly dust the pasta and then pass each log through a cavatelli roller.

To assemble Bring a large pot of salted water to a boil over high heat, add the pasta and cook for 45 seconds. Drain and add to the sauce. Stir in the Parmesan. Divide the warm pasta among individual bowls and garnish with extra ricotta.

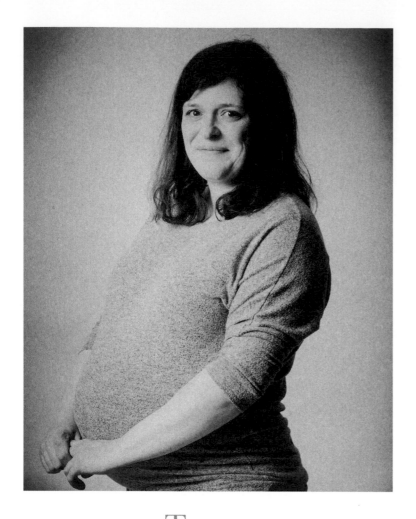

Tapeo

— chef —
MARIE-FLEUR
SAINT-PIERRE

More than ten years ago, servers Victor Afonso and Sébastien Muniz opened a Spanish tapas bar in the Villeray neighbourhood of Montreal and brought in Chef Marie-Fleur Saint-Pierre to helm the kitchen. Disciplined and passionate, she experiments extensively with her ingredients, and the result is a wide-ranging menu of hot (*calientes*) and cold (*frias*) small plates. A large blackboard lists their many offerings, from local fish and seafood to Iberian meats, and the savoury compositions for which the restaurant is best known.

During the day, the dining room is flooded with natural light from the large front windows, and at night, the soft glow from the streetlights and the interior pendants creates a warm atmosphere. But it's the food that has dedicated diners like us making the trek with our friends in tow. It's a fun place to have a rewarding meal with a large group and sample from among many favourites such as the fresh sardine salad, the sweet and salty bacon-wrapped scallops and the juicy grilled chorizo. Chef Marie-Fleur's smoky duck carpaccio is a great recipe to impress your friends, and the *fideos salmorra* will transport you to Sevilla and leave you singing her praises. And lucky for us, we can relive another Chef Marie-Fleur experience at their second restaurant, Mesón, a few blocks away.

Salmorra

3 dried ancho chilies, stemmed, seeded and rehydrated in 1 cup of hot water (reserve ¼ cup of the soaking water)
2 ripe Roma tomatoes, roughly chopped
6 garlic cloves, peeled
1 Tbsp olive oil
1 Tbsp sherry vinegar
1 Tbsp white sugar
1 tsp smoked paprika
salt to taste

Parsley oil

½ bunch fresh parsley, roughly chopped
1 small shallot, roughly chopped
¼ cup vegetable oil
1 tsp piri-piri sauce or your favourite hot sauce
1 ½ tsp sherry vinegar
salt to taste

Aïoli

1 large egg
1 Tbsp Dijon mustard
2 Tbsp fresh lemon juice
1 garlic clove
1 cup vegetable oil
1 to 2 Tbsp ice water
salt

Fideos

1 Tbsp olive oil
2 garlic cloves, minced
1 ½ cups chopped raw shrimp
1 cup finely sliced Iberian chorizo sausage
2 cups cod or other firm, white fish, cut into cubes
salt to taste
1 cup salmorra (recipe here)
4 cups filini pasta (or capellini, broken into 1- to 2-inch pieces), cooked al dente
2 to 3 cups fish stock
2 Tbsp sherry vinegar
½ cup aïoli (recipe here)
¼ cup parsley oil (recipe here)
1 lemon, cut into 4 to 6 wedges

Serves 4 to 6

Fideos Salmorra

Fideos is very thin pasta, like a spaghettini, and *salmorra* is a smoky tomato-garlic sauce similar to the one used in paella. This recipe makes more aïoli than you'll need, but you'll want lots on hand for your guests or to serve with other fish, meat or vegetable dishes. What dish isn't improved with a little garlicky mayonnaise?

Salmorra Place all of the ingredients, including the ¼ cup of the ancho soaking water, in a blender and process at high speed until smooth. Will keep refrigerated in an airtight container for up to 7 days.

Parsley oil Place all of the ingredients in a blender and process at high speed until smooth. Will keep refrigerated in an airtight container for up to 2 days.

Aïoli Place the egg, mustard, lemon juice and garlic in a blender and process at medium speed. With the motor running, slowly add the vegetable oil in a thin stream until the aïoli is emulsified. Add the ice water and process until smooth. Season with salt. Will keep refrigerated in an airtight container for up to 2 days.

Fideos Heat the olive oil in a large sauté pan over high heat. Stir in the garlic, shrimp, chorizo and cod and season with salt. Add the 1 cup salmorra, making sure to cover all the ingredients in the pan. Pour in the pasta, the fish stock and the vinegar, increase the heat to maximum and cook until the liquid has been completely absorbed, 5 to 7 minutes.

To serve, preheat the broiler. Divide the fideos evenly among 4 ovenproof terracotta plates. Broil for 45 to 60 seconds to obtain a nice crust on top. Garnish with aïoli, parsley oil and a wedge of lemon. Serve immediately with extra aïoli on the side.

½ cup blond beer
¼ cup smoked salt
¼ cup white sugar
1 bay leaf, crushed
2 small boneless duck breasts,
   skin on, each 12 to 14 oz
½ cup BBQ sauce (see below)
1 cup frisée lettuce or watercress
¼ chopped toasted hazelnuts
½ cup finely grated Manchego cheese
2 Tbsp chopped fresh chives
cracked black pepper
olive oil

½ cup ketchup
½ cup water
2 Tbsp quince jelly
2 Tbsp sherry vinegar
¼ onion, chopped
salt and black pepper
1 ½ tsp piri-piri sauce (or your
   favourite hot sauce)
1 Tbsp truffle paste

Smoky Duck Carpaccio, Truffle and Quince BBQ Sauce

Serves 4 to 6

Start this dish a couple of days before you plan to serve it so that the duck has time to marinate before being cooked. Look for piri-piri sauce, quince jelly and truffle paste in specialty gourmet shops.

Smoky duck carpaccio In a bowl large enough to hold the duck breasts, gently mix the beer, smoked salt, sugar and bay leaf until you have a nice paste. Add the duck and use your hands to completely cover the breasts with the paste. When they are well coated, place one duck breast on top of the other to form a sandwich. Wrap tightly in plastic wrap and refrigerate for 48 hours.

BBQ sauce Place all of the ingredients in a medium pot over medium heat, bring to a boil, reduce the heat to medium and cook for 20 minutes. Transfer the mixture to a blender and process at high speed until smooth. Allow to cool to room temperature. Will keep refrigerated in an airtight container for up to 1 month or frozen indefinitely.

Finish duck carpaccio Rinse the duck breasts under cold, running water. Pat them dry with paper towels.

Heat a sauté pan over medium heat, add the duck breasts, skin side down, and sear until dark golden and crisp, 6 to 8 minutes. Turn the duck over and cook for 1 minute more. Remove from the heat and allow the meat to rest for 10 minutes. Using a very sharp knife, slice the meat as thinly as possible.

To serve, divide the sliced duck among the individual plates, arranging it in a single layer. Garnish with a couple of tablespoonfuls of BBQ sauce. Arrange the frisée lettuce (or watercress), hazelnuts and cheese on top of the meat and sprinkle with the chives. Season with some cracked pepper and a drizzle of olive oil.

Tavern
on the Square

—— *chef* ——

STEPHEN LESLIE

Stephen Leslie is the chef and co-owner of long-time favourite Monkland Tavern and the recent Le Sieur d'Iberville as well as Tavern on the Square. Like many locals, we've been coming to this below-ground restaurant on the edge of Westmount for years, drawn again and again by the meatball appetizer, crispy candied shrimp and perfectly cooked salmon. The ingredients are always fresh and local, prepared in a southern Italian style with impeccable classical French technique. And the atmosphere is like being at a dinner party with old friends— guests circulate from table to table greeting each other and calling the staff by their first name.

Born and raised in Montreal, Stephen studied culinary arts in Vancouver, apprenticed with Umberto Menghi at Il Giardino and returned home to open his restaurants. While most restaurant kitchens now open into the dining room, Stephen and his crew are hidden away in the back. But there's lots going on out front, with seating on various levels, from banquettes and couches to tables and the bar. It's a design that encourages conversation and gives a great view of the room. In recent years, Stephen has added to the classic menu, introducing an exciting table d'hôte menu that show-cases his passion for food and reminds us why we keep coming back for more.

facing ROAST CHICKEN WITH SMOKED
OYSTER AND SAUSAGE STUFFING

Brined chicken

8 cups water
juice and zest of 1 lemon
4 bay leaves
½ bunch fresh parsley
2 sprigs fresh rosemary
4 garlic cloves, unpeeled but crushed
2 tsp smoked paprika
1 Tbsp black peppercorns
3 Tbsp brown sugar
½ cup kosher salt
1 whole chicken, 3 to 3½ lbs, trussed
¼ cup melted butter

Smoked oyster and sausage stuffing

8 to 10 Tbsp olive oil
1 onion, diced
2 celery stalks, diced
2 Italian sausages, casings removed
½ lb button mushrooms, quartered
¾ lb portobello mushrooms, cut in large dice
2 frozen porcini mushrooms, thawed and diced (or use dried porcini, but roast them in the oven and then grind them in a spice grinder)
salt and pepper
½ cup grated cheddar
½ cup grated Parmesan
1 loaf brioche or stale bread, coarsely chopped
½ cup whipping cream
2 large eggs, beaten
¼ bunch fresh flat-leaf parsley, chopped
½ tsp salt
½ tsp black pepper
2 garlic cloves, chopped
1 can smoked oysters, undrained

Roast Chicken with Smoked Oyster and Sausage Stuffing

Serves eight

I use a variation of Thomas Keller's chicken brine for this recipe. At the restaurant we debone and stuff our chickens, but you'll cook them separately here. We also like to sauté Brussels sprouts leaves in the chicken drippings and serve them with a slice of stuffing. Start the recipe a full day ahead so the chicken has time to brine before you cook it. Remove the chickens from the brine and pat them dry when you put the stuffing in the oven to cook. This step allows the chicken to come to room temperature so it cooks faster and more evenly.

Brined chicken Place the water, lemon juice and zest, bay leaves, parsley, rosemary, garlic, paprika, pepper, sugar and salt in a large stockpot big enough to hold the chicken. Bring the brine to a boil over high heat, boil for 2 minutes and then remove from the heat and allow to cool. Immerse the chickens in the brine and refrigerate, covered, for 24 hours.

Smoked oyster and sausage stuffing Preheat the oven to 350°F. Lightly oil a 5 × 9-inch nonstick loaf pan.

Heat a large sauté pan over medium-high heat. Add 3 Tbsp of the olive oil, then add the onions and celery and sauté until soft and translucent, about 3 minutes. Transfer the sautéed vegetables to a large bowl and set aside.

Return the pan to the heat and add another 2 Tbsp of olive oil. Add the sausages, breaking them up with a wooden spoon until the meat is fully cooked, about 5 minutes. Add the button, portobello and porcini mushrooms and the remaining 3 to 5 Tbsp olive oil, and cook for 5 minutes or until the mushrooms are soft. Season with salt and pepper and add the sausages and mushrooms to the onion mixture.

Stir the cheddar and Parmesan cheeses, the bread, cream, eggs, parsley, salt and pepper, garlic and smoked oysters into the onion-sausage mixture. Spoon the stuffing into the loaf pan and cook for 1 hour. It should be firm to the touch.

Finish brined chicken Preheat the oven to 450°F.

Place the chicken on a wire rack set inside a roasting pan (you want air to be able to circulate under the chicken). Using a pastry brush, baste the chicken with melted butter, then roast it in the oven for 20 minutes. Reduce the heat to 400°F and cook for another 50 minutes, or until the internal temperature of the meat reaches 160°F. Test the temperature by inserting a meat thermometer into the thickest part of the meat near the thigh. Remove the chicken from the oven, set it on a carving board and tent it (or cover) with aluminum foil. Allow to rest for 30 to 35 minutes before carving.

2 to 3 shallots, finely diced
1 cup red wine vinegar
1 cup canola oil
1 cup olive oil
1 Tbsp white sugar
1 Tbsp + 1¼ tsp kosher salt
½ Tbsp ground black pepper

Pickled onions
2 red onions, julienned
½ cup red wine vinegar
½ cup cider vinegar
1 cup water
2 Tbsp coarse salt
¼ cup white sugar
½ Tbsp black pepper
½ Tbsp coriander seeds
½ Tbsp fennel seeds
2 bay leaves

Fall/Winter Vegetable Salad

Serves 4 to 6

This salad makes a nice alternative to lettuce greens, especially in the cold winter months when lettuce is expensive and not good! This salad is a bit of work prepping the ingredients, but the results are fully worth it. As the seasons change, so can your vegetables. Jerusalem artichokes, also called sunchokes, are available in the fall at farmers' markets and good produce stores.

Red wine vinaigrette Place all of the ingredients in a mason jar and shake well until combined. Will keep refrigerated in an airtight container for up to 2 weeks.

Pickled onions Place the onions in a large heatproof bowl.

In a medium pot, combine all the remaining ingredients and bring to a boil over high heat. Set a fine-mesh sieve over the onions and strain the pickling liquid through it. Discard the solids. Allow the onions to cool at room temperature or in the fridge. Will keep refrigerated in an airtight container for up to 1 week.

Vegetable salad Preheat the oven to 400°F. Have ready 3 large squares of aluminum foil.

Separate the different types of beets. Wrap each variety in a separate sheet of foil, and roast them all in the oven until tender, about 1 hour. They are done when a wooden skewer inserted in the flesh comes out easily. Remove from the oven and allow to cool. Leave the oven on.

Line a baking sheet with parchment paper. Scrub the skin of the delicata squash (it is edible) or peel the butternut squash. Cut the squash in half, remove and discard the seeds and cut the flesh into ⅛ to ¼-inch-thick slices. Place the squash in a large bowl, add the olive oil, season with salt and pepper and toss well. Arrange the squash in a single layer on the baking sheet and roast in the oven

Vegetable salad

4 assorted medium beets, ideally yellow, red and Chioggia
1 delicata or butternut squash
¼ cup olive oil
salt and black pepper
juice from 1 lemon (optional)
5 Jerusalem artichokes
10 Brussels sprouts, trimmed and cut in half
¼ bunch kale, cut in 1-inch dice

3 to 4 radishes, thinly sliced on a mandolin
2 heirloom carrots (preferably Nantes), peeled and thinly sliced on a mandolin
1 apple, peeled, cored and julienned
2 Tbsp pickled red onions
2 Tbsp pumpkin seeds, toasted
2 Tbsp almond slivers or slices, toasted

for 12 minutes. If they are beginning to burn, reduce the heat. If not, continue to roast them for another 3 to 8 minutes, until tender. Remove from the oven and set aside. Leave the oven on.

Using your hands, peel and discard the skins from the beets. Place the red beets in a small bowl, and the others in a separate bowl. Add 3 to 4 Tbsp of the red wine vinaigrette to each bowl and toss well. Set aside.

Line a baking sheet with parchment paper. Fill a large bowl with water and lemon juice. Scrub the Jerusalem artichokes well to remove any dirt. Using a mandolin, slice the artichokes $1/16$ to ⅛ inch thick. (If you are not cooking them right away, fill a large bowl with water and lemon juice, and place the Jerusalem artichokes in it to prevent them from turning brown.) Arrange the artichoke slices in a single layer on the baking sheet and roast them in the oven for 15 to 20 minutes. Remove from the oven and set aside.

Fill a small bowl with ice water. Bring a small pot of salted water to a boil over high heat. Add the Brussels sprouts and blanch for 30 seconds. Using a slotted spoon, transfer the Brussels sprouts to the ice water to stop the cooking and preserve their colour. Add the kale to the boiling water and blanch for 60 seconds. Drain and immediately add the kale to the ice water. Using your hands, transfer the kale and Brussels sprouts to a clean bowl, gently squeezing out any excess water.

To assemble Place all of the vegetables (including the radishes and carrots) along with the apple and the pickled onions into a large salad bowl, being careful to remove any excess water. Toss with enough vinaigrette to coat lightly. Season with a small pinch of salt and pepper. Sprinkle with pumpkin seeds and almonds to finish. Serve immediately.

Metric Conversion Charts

Volume

Imperial	Metric
⅛ tsp	0.5 mL
¼ tsp	1 mL
½ tsp	2.5 mL
¾ tsp	4 mL
1 tsp	5 mL
½ Tbsp	8 mL
1 Tbsp	15 mL
1½ Tbsp	23 mL
2 Tbsp	30 mL
¼ cup	60 mL
⅓ cup	80 mL
½ cup	125 mL
⅔ cup	165 mL
¾ cup	185 mL
1 cup	250 mL
1¼ cups	310 mL
1⅓ cups	330 mL
1½ cups	375 mL
1⅔ cups	415 mL
1¾ cups	435 mL
2 cups	500 mL
2 ¼ cups	560 mL
2 ⅓ cups	580 mL
2 ½ cups	625 mL
2 ¾ cups	690 mL
3 cups	750 mL
4 cups / 1 qt	1 L
5 cups	1.25 L
6 cups	1.5 L
7 cups	1.75 L
8 cups	2 L

Weight

Imperial	Metric
½ oz	15 g
1 oz	30 g
2 oz	60 g
3 oz	85 g
4 oz (¼ lb)	115 g
5 oz	140 g
6 oz	170 g
7 oz	200 g
8 oz (½ lb)	225 g
9 oz	255 g
10 oz	285 g
11 oz	310 g
12 oz (¾ lb)	340 g
13 oz	370 g
14 oz	400 g
15 oz	425 g
16 oz (1 lb)	450 g
1¼ lbs	570 g
1½ lbs	670 g
2 lbs	900 g
3 lbs	1.4 kg
4 lbs	1.8 kg
5 lbs	2.3 kg
6 lbs	2.7 kg

Liquid measures (for alcohol)

Imperial	Metric
1 fl oz	30 mL
2 fl oz	60 mL
3 fl oz	90 mL
4 fl oz	120 mL

Cans and jars

Imperial	Metric
6 oz	170 g
28 oz	796 mL

Linear

Imperial	Metric
⅛ inch	3 mm
¼ inch	6 mm
½ inch	12 mm
¾ inch	2 cm
1 inch	2.5 cm
1¼ inches	3 cm
1½ inches	3.5 cm
1¾ inches	4.5 cm
2 inches	5 cm
2 ½ inches	6.5 cm
3 inches	7.5 cm
4 inches	10 cm
5 inches	12.5 cm
6 inches	15 cm
7 inches	18 cm
10 inches	25 cm
12 inches / 1 foot	30 cm
13 inches	33 cm
16 inches	41 cm
18 inches	46 cm
24 inches / 2 feet	60 cm
28 inches	70 cm
30 inches	75 cm
6 feet	1.8 m

Temperature

Imperial	Metric
90°F	32°C
120°F	49°C
125°F	52°C
130°F	54°C
140°F	60°C
150°F	66°C
155°F	68°C
160°F	71°C
165°F	74°C
170°F	77°C
175°F	80°C
180°F	82°C
190°F	88°C
200°F	93°C
240°F	116°C
250°F	121°C
300°F	149°C
325°F	163°C
350°F	177°C
360°F	182°C
375°F	191°C

Oven temperature

Imperial	Metric
200°F	95°C
250°F	120°C
275°F	135°C
300°F	150°C
325°F	160°C
350°F	180°C
375°F	190°C
400°F	200°C
425°F	220°C
450°F	230°C

Acknowledgements

We would like to thank Chris Labonté of Figure 1 for making that first phone call to Appetite for Books. Thanks to Lucy Kenward and Grace Yaginuma for tirelessly editing our jumbled words and the chefs' recipes and to Jessica Sullivan for overseeing the visual and creative direction of the book.

For the beautiful photographs, we want to thank Fabrice Gaëtan (www.fabrice gaetan.com) and his assistant François Bouchard for having the eye to bring all the recipes to life on the page, and Sarah Laroche from Very Much (www. verymuch.ca) for pairing the perfect styles with the food.

Thanks to all the chefs who accepted our request to be included in this book. Your passion for representing Montreal is shown on every page. We are also grateful to Gail Simmons for having a strong affection for Montreal and the restaurants here.

We are delighted that the 1940s cast-iron pan given to Tays by her great-aunt Margie, and in which Tays made her first meals in her first kitchen, appears on the cover of our book. And, finally, thanks to Nate for putting up with Mom and Dad while they debated about what restaurant to eat at next.

JONATHAN + TAYS

Index

red chilies, in confit grape tomatoes, 9
red chilies, in Szechwan-style poached "white fish," 59
red chili / tuna / Meyer lemon / salsa verde, 148–49
Szechwan chilies, in Szechwan-style poached "white fish," 59

ICE CREAM AND SORBET
buttermilk ice cream, 213
ricotta sorbet, 55
Icelandic cod, borlotti beans, collards and tomato sauce, 53
Italian sausages. *See under* sausage(s)

JAM
stained glass, *195,* 196–97
tomato, 6
jelly, grapefruit, 68
JERUSALEM ARTICHOKES
confit, sunflower seed butter, northern spiced rum raisins and green bean and apple salad, 140–41
in fall/winter vegetable salad, 240–41

kale, in fall/winter vegetable salad, 240–41

labneh, 136
latkes, Nana's, *74,* 78–79
LEEK(S)
in Argentinean puchero, 112
ash, 144
LEMON
bars, *210,* 211
juice, in ponzu sauce, 181
mostarda, 148
sour cream, 202
in stained glass jam, 196–97
LETTUCE
frisée, in salmon beet gravlax, 22–23
frisée, in smoky duck carpaccio, 235
romaine, in Ferreira Caesar salad, *50,* 51
LIVER
spread, toasted bagels with, 186
monkfish, torchon with ponzu sauce, 180–81
LOBSTER
in Ferreira Caesar salad, 51
steamed, 157–59, *160*
London tea party, 27

macerated grapes, 16
Manchego, in smoky duck carpaccio, 235
MAPLE
-glazed pork belly, carrot pancake and pickled carrots, 184–85
in glazed vegetables, 137–39
in marinated raisins, 141
-mustard glazed pork belly with endives, 16–17
in ponzu sauce, 181
sugar financiers, 189
in sunflower butter, 140–41
in sushi rice, 178
syrup, Bremner pancakes with, 24
in tzimmes, 166–67
in yuzu cream, 101
marinated black cod, 222–23
marinated grilled bell peppers, 144
marinated raisins, 141
marinated red onions, 186
marrow, bone, with potato purée and mullet caviar, 82–83
mascarpone, in gnocchi, 145–47
mashed potatoes, 46–47
meatballs, 99
MEATS. *See also* bacon; beef; chicken; pork; poultry; sausage(s); veal
elk tataki, 220–21
rabbit boudin blanc, 84–87
Medjool date purée, 215
Meyer lemon, in lemon mostarda, 148
MIGNONETTE. *See also* dressings and vinaigrettes
classic, 161
spicy vinegar, 161
milanesa de pollo con queso (breaded chicken cutlets with cheese), *109,* 110–11
MINT
in barley salad with mixed herbs, goji berries and pine nuts, 13
in best chicken noodle soup ever, 175
in cataplana de marisco (seafood bouillabaisse), 49
in salsa verde, 148
Minus 8 caramel, 214
MISO
black cod glazed with, 31
-braised carrots, 215
in salmon (or tuna) tartare, 178–79
and tamari-marinated black cod, 222–24
-yuzu sauce, 101

Moishes' steak, *151,* 152–53
mole sauce, 92–93
monkfish liver torchon with ponzu sauce, 180–81
mozzarella, in quesadilla all dressed, 62–63
mullet caviar and potato purée, bone marrow with, 82–83
MUSHROOM(S)
button, in crab gratin on toast, 18
chanterelle, veal sweetbreads with, 70–72
hedgehog, and spaghetti squash and Brussels sprouts in cedar butter, 136–39
morel, rabbit boudin blanc with, 84–87
porcini, in smoked oyster and sausage stuffing, 238–39
portobello, in smoked oyster and sausage stuffing, 238–39
shiitake, broth, 222
shiitake, sautéed, miso- and tamari-marinated black cod with, 222–24
wood ear, salad with walnuts, 57, *58*
mussels, in cataplana de marisco (seafood bouillabaisse), 49
MUSTARD
in lemon mostarda, 148
-maple glaze, 16
seeds, pickled, 214

Nana's latkes, *74,* 78–79
Nashville hot pig's ears, 36–39, *38*
noodles, Filipino fried, 107.
See also pasta
NORI
paste, 103
for salmon (or tuna) oshizushi, 178–79
NUTS AND SEEDS. *See also* almond(s); pumpkin seeds
hazelnuts, in smoky duck carpaccio, 235
pine nuts, mixed herbs and goji berries, barley salad with, 13
pistachios, in cauliflower spätzle, 168–69
sunflower butter, 140
walnuts, wood ear mushroom salad with, 57

OCTOPUS
in cataplana de marisco (seafood bouillabaisse), 49
mole tacos, 91–93